Strategic Marketing Planning

Malcolm McDonald

Cranfield
School of Management

KOGAN
PAGE

First published in 1992
Reprinted 1993

Kogan Page Ltd
120 Pentonville Road
London N1 9JN

British Library Cataloguing in Publication Data
A CIP record of this book is available from the British Library.

ISBN 0 7494 0767 0

Typeset by Books Unlimited (Nottm), Sutton-in-Ashfield, Notts. NG17 1AL
Printed in England by Clays Ltd., St Ives plc

Strategic Marketing Planning

1

Professor Malcolm HB McDonald
MA (Oxon), MSc, PhD, FCIM FRSA

Malcolm is Professor of Planning and Chairman of the International Marketing Planning Centre at the Cranfield School of Management.

He is a graduate in English Language and Literature from Oxford University, in Business Studies from Bradford University Management Centre, and has a PhD from the Cranfield Institute of Technology. He has extensive industrial experience, including a number of years as Marketing Director of Canada Dry.

In the past ten years he has run seminars and workshops on Marketing Planning in the UK, Europe, India, the Far East, Australia and the US.

He has written twenty books, including the best seller *Market Plans; how to prepare them; how to use them* (Butterworth-Heinemann, 1989), and many of his papers have been published. He is editor of International Marketing Review.

His current interests centre around the development of computer based training programs in marketing and the development of expert systems in marketing planning.

CONTENTS

5

LIST OF FIGURES

LIST OF TABLES

THE CRANFIELD MANAGEMENT RESEARCH SERIES

The Cranfield Management Research Series represents an exciting joint initiative between the Cranfield School of Management and Kogan Page.

As one of Europe's leading post-graduate business schools, Cranfield is renowned for its applied research activities, which cover a wide range of issues relating to the practice of management.

Each title in the Series is based on current research and authored by Cranfield faculty or their associates. Many of the research projects have been undertaken with the sponsorship and active assistance of organisations from the industrial, commercial or public sectors. The aim of the Series is to make the findings of direct relevance to managers through texts which are academically sound, accessible and practical.

For managers and academics alike, the Cranfield Management Research Series will provide access to up-to-date management thinking from some of Europe's leading academics and practitioners. The series represents both Cranfield's and Kogan Page's commitment to furthering the improvement of management practice in all types of organisations.

THE SERIES EDITORS

Frank Fishwick
Reader in Managerial Economics
Director of Admissions at Cranfield School of Management

Frank joined Cranfield from Aston University in 1966, having previously worked in textiles, electronics and local government (town and country planning). Recent research and consultancy interests have been focused on business concentration, competition policy and the book publishing industry. He has been directing a series of research studies for the

Commission of the European Communities, working in collaboration with business economists in France and Germany. Frank is permanent economic adviser to the Publishers Association in the UK and is a regular consultant to other public and private sector organisations in the UK, continental Europe and the US.

Gerry Johnson
Professor of Strategic Management
Director of the Centre for Strategic Management and Organisational Change
Director of Research at Cranfield School of Management

After graduating from University College London, Gerry worked for several years in management positions in Unilever and Reed International before becoming a Management Consultant. Since 1976, he has taught at Aston University Management Centre, Management Business School, and from 1988 at Cranfield School of Management. His research work is primarily concerned with processes of strategic decision making and strategic change in organisations. He also works as a consultant on issues of strategy formulation change at a senior level with a number of UK and international firms.

Shaun Tyson
Professor of Human Resource Management
Director of the Human Resource Research Centre
Dean of the Faculty of Management and Administration at Cranfield School of Management

Shaun studied at London University and spent eleven years in senior positions in industry within engineering and electronic companies.

For four years he was a lecturer in personnel management at the Civil Service College, and joined Cranfield in 1979. He has acted as a consultant and researched widely into human resource strategies, policies and the evaluation of the function. He has published eight books.

PREFACE

Already, the 1990s have forced dramatic changes in the ways organisations think, plan and behave. What caused success in the 1980s no longer worked towards the end of that decade, and those who clung doggedly to earlier policies disappeared with a suddenness and viciousness undreamed of in calmer times.

It wasn't just the growth of competition from the Pacific Rim countries, nor the ageing and declining populations of many parts of Europe. Nor was it the speed with which new technologies could be developed and commercialised and then transferred to less developed countries. More than anything else, it was rapidly changing consumer attitudes towards many of the things that had been taken for granted hitherto. The more sophisticated and environmentally aware consumers began to exercise their power, and individual life-styles, combined with technological breakthroughs that enabled institutions to offer more personal choice, challenged for the first time the long-established tenets of mass marketing.

This, combined with the sudden emergence of the concept of the single European market, had such a dramatic impact on all the established theories of management that some of the more traditional books on business management started to look increasingly suspect in this new, more chaotic and uncertain environment. On careful reflection, however, it became clear that the more fundamental tenets outlined in books on business strategy were still applicable in the 1990s, providing some effort could be applied in tailoring them to the new challenges raised by the new consumer and the new market in Europe.

The purpose of this book is quite simply to explain the concepts of strategic marketing and how to apply them to the new challenges facing organisations in the 1990s. In my years of consulting and in management education, there has appeared to be a substantial gap between theory and practice, even in the marketing field, where much of the theory has developed from observations of practice. I have reached a number of conclusions:

- the now large number of strategic concepts and principles that evolved during the 1980s are not widely known or their application understood;
- faced with an increasing number of concepts that are potentially relevant to any marketing strategy, it is not clear which are the ones to apply;
- a relatively simple, but practical, framework is necessary for the decision-maker or the strategist to understand the essence of what is required, so that the appropriate concepts and techniques are used.

This book is an attempt to address some of these issues, which have been written about by the author during recent years. This book is simply a compendium of some of these papers, each of which has been carefully selected to represent a major issue current to marketing practioners.

The primary target of this book is marketing executives and students of marketing and business strategy courses. It should also be useful, however, to multinational corporations and foreign companies seeking to understand marketing strategy and the evolution and performance of businesses operating in a variety of markets.

The first chapter provides an overview of competitive marketing ¬trategy concepts and principles and presents a practical framework for identifying competitive position and the strategies necessary to develop, maintain or defend it. Chapter 2 examines strategic marketing planning as a process. It looks at what it is and how to do it. Chapter 3 takes up the theme introduced in Chapter 2 and consists of a state-of-the-art review of strategic marketing planning. This is in contrast to Chapter 1, which examines a whole range of strategic marketing planning concepts, structures and frameworks. Chapter 4 examines strategic marketing planning in its organisational context. In particular, corporate culture is explored. The fifth chapter is concerned with state-of-the-art developments in strategic marketing planning and information technology. In particular, expert systems are explored. The final chapter suggests some future scenarios for strategic marketing planning.

Professor Malcolm McDonald
Cranfield School of Management
September 1992

ACKNOWLEDGEMENTS

A book of this type requires the help of many people. To all those executives who provided information and time, I am deeply indebted. I wish to thank them and their colleagues for their involvement and contributions. In particular, I should also like to thank Dr Linden Brown for his valuable advice and for his permission to publish Chapter 1 of this book. Also, to Hugh Wilson and John Leppard, for their contributions to other chapters in this book, I express my thanks.

Professor Malcolm McDonald
Cranfield School of Management

1

Competitive Marketing Strategy: Concepts and Application*

This book is about competitive advantage – establishing, building, defending and maintaining it – and the strategies required to do that in a competitive environment. What those strategies should be will depend upon an organisation's existing competitive position, where it wants to be in the future, its capabilities and the competitive market environment it faces. The pertinent concepts are explored and their application examined in the European context by example, illustration and case study.

THE TASK OF COMPETITIVE MARKETING STRATEGY

Effective action is preceded by four interrelated steps: audit, objectives, strategies and plans for implementation. Following a situation review, objectives specify what is to be achieved, usually in terms of revenue, profit and market share. Strategies set out the route that has been chosen – the means for achieving the objectives. Plans for implementation provide the vehicle for getting to the destination along the chosen route.

In a competitive environment, the starting point is to identify the competitive position, set business objectives, which will comprise revenue, market share and profit requirements, then formulate the

---

* This chapter is reproduced by kind permission of Dr Linden Brown of the University of New South Wales, Australia. An earlier version of this paper appears in Dr Linden Brown's book *Competitive Marketing Strategy: developing, maintaining and defending competitive position*. Published by Thomas Nelson, Australia, 1990.

strategies necessary to achieve the new position. Under these conditions, marketing strategies are the centrepiece.

The task of competitive marketing strategy is to move a business from its present position to a stronger competitive one. This must be done by adapting and responding to external trends and forces such as competition, market changes and technology and developing and matching corporate resources and capabilities with the firm's opportunities (see Figure 1.1). Recognition of the complexity of this task, especially for large diversified companies, has led to the development of theories, concepts and techniques that prescribe the process of strategy formulation in a systematic manner. This has become known as the strategic planning process.

Figure 1.1 Strategies to achieve future position

THE STRATEGIC PLANNING PROCESS

Strategic planning is the process of formulating longer-term objectives and strategies for the entire business or business unit by matching its resources with its opportunities. Its purpose is to help a business to set and reach realistic objectives and achieve a desired competitive position within a defined time. It aims to reduce the risk of error and place the business in a situation in which it can anticipate change, respond to it, and even create change to its advantage.

Evolution of the process

In the 1960s, strategic planning (known then as corporate planning) was essentially a financial plan of the business extrapolated from a base year. It worked well as a planning tool when demand exceeded supply, markets were growing and external change was minimal. When major external changes hit companies and industries in the late-1960s and the 1970s, however, this type of planning was no longer adequate. The successful challenge to retail price maintenance, for example, changed the nature of the food manufacturing industry, and the lowering of tariffs and provision of import quotas on many categories of goods changed local industries.

Increasing competition, more demanding customers and changing markets have forced more commitment to marketing to enable firms to capitalise on competitive advantages. Some companies now manage resources, markets and competition through a multi-level system of objectives and strategies.

Aaker depicts the evolution of management systems.[1] The final stage is a strategic market management approach in which the firm adopts a planning and review process that aims to cope with strategic surprises and fast developing threats and opportunities. This is shown in Table 1.1.

In response to changing external factors such as technology and market maturity, firms changed their products and markets, sold and acquired businesses and reorganised. This required them to redefine their business scope because of the need to commit resources to new businesses and market development. Courtaulds, for example, originally in textiles, is now in paints and industrial plastics, and ICI, originally in bulk chemicals, is in pharmaceuticals and the banks are in insurance and financial services. Allied Breweries is in hotels and leisure centres and W H Smith is in DIY.

Steps in the process

In reality, firms adopt a hybrid of management systems depending upon their size, diversity, position in the market, rate and type of external change, resource commitments and management attitudes to planning.

Table 1.1 Evolution of management systems

	Budgeting/ control	*Long-range planning*	*Strategic planning*	*Strategic market management*
Management emphasis	Control deviations and manage complexity	Anticipate growth and manage complexity	Change strategic thrust and capability	Cope with strategic surprises and fast-developing threats/ opportunities
Assumptions	The past repeats	Past trends will continue	New trends and discontinuities are predictable	Planning cycles inadequate to deal with rapid changes
The Process	← ———————— Periodic ———————————→ Real Time			
Time period associated with system	From 1990s	From 1950s	From 1960s	From mid-1970s

Source: Aaker, D A (1984) *Strategic Market Management,* Wiley, p 11.

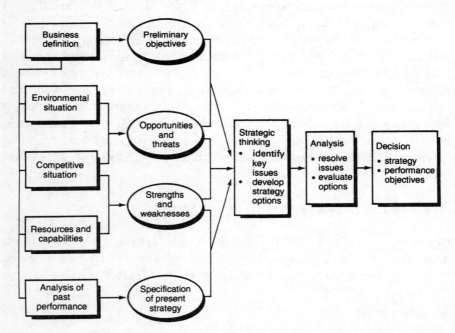

Figure 1.2 Strategy formulation process
Source: Day, G S (1984) *Strategic Market Planning,* West Publishing, p 49

What is important, however, is to recognise that a series of systematic steps can be useful in formulating strategies when the stakes are high and the resource commitment is significant to the firm. It reduces the risk of leaving out key issues, and it highlights the assumptions on which strategies are based and resources committed. A series of interrelated steps are involved in formulating strategies. Day shows a typical strategy formulation process in Figure 1.2.[2]

The basic steps are:

- business definition – scope of planning activities;
- situation assessment – analysis of internal and environmental factors;
- preliminary performance objectives – based on past performance and initial corporate expectations, constrained by achievement reality;
- strategic development – identification and evaluation of strategic options and choice of an option;
- implementation – includes action programmes, functional budgets and timetables; and
- monitoring of performance against objectives.

In essence, an analysis of internal and external factors helps to develop the business definition, relative competitive advantage and broad objectives. The central issues must be identified, the strategy options set out and evaluated. Strategic decisions are taken by selecting the strategy and relevant performance objectives. Aaker expands some of the elements in this process.[3]

The analyses by Day and Aaker relate primarily to strategy development for the strategic business unit ('SBU'). McDonald[4] looks at planning from a more highly focused marketing perspective and views the marketing planning process within a corporate framework. They see the steps as:

- corporate (business) objectives;
- marketing audit – analyses of external environment and internal elements, including the marketing mix;
- SWOT analysis (ie of strengths, weaknesses, opportunities and threats) and planning assumptions, including key determinants of marketing success or failure;
- marketing objectives and strategies, including objectives for products and markets and strategies for each part of the marketing mix;
- programmes containing details of timing, responsibilities and costs, with sales forecasts and budget; and
- measurement and review.

The development of competitive marketing strategies needs to draw from both perspectives. The SBU level provides tools of strategic analysis that are applicable to the development of marketing strategies and cut across the whole business. The functional marketing level helps define the elements that make up a marketing strategy for each of the product lines and market segments. Specific brand positioning and marketing mix decisions become more narrowly defined at the product market level of analysis. The SBU level provides tools of strategic marketing analysis, while the functional marketing level helps define the elements that make up a marketing strategy.

The planning process and conceptual analysis

There is a considerable number of strategic analysis concepts, methods and techniques from which to draw guidelines for competitive marketing strategies. The problem is to determine which are the most useful and relevant. It is important to recognise that each concept or technique provides only part of the picture and should not be relied upon as the only guide to strategy formulation. These concepts have evolved from the field of marketing, and in recent years, the area of strategic planning.

Much of the literature focuses on competitive analyses[5] as the key to identifying competitive advantages, and on the need to develop global strategies such as those that have been successfully implemented by Japanese corporations.[6] Many attempt to provide guidelines and general principles for the selection of strategies under different conditions. Indeed, the links between strategy and performance have been the subject of detailed statistical analysis by the Strategic Planning Institute.[7] The PIMS Project identified six major links from studies of more than 2600 businesses. From this analysis, principles have been derived for the selection of different strategies depending upon industry type, market conditions and competitive position of the business.

A reaction against theoretical approaches to strategic planning has occurred in recent years, however, with particular focus on the limitations of portfolio planning.[8] Some writers argue that there are no valid generalisations about strategy and criticise strategy consultants, who, they claim, have misled managers by making recommendations based on excessively broad principles. Lubatkin and Pitts[9] compare a 'policy perspective' with the 'PIMS perspective'. They suggest that a policy perspective assumes that no two businesses are exactly alike and therefore there are few specific formulae for achieving competitive advantage. They suggest that the PIMS perspective involves a mechanistic application of formulae to complex management problems, resulting in potentially misleading prescriptions for strategy.

What is agreed, however, is that strategic planning represents a useful process by which an organisation formulates its strategies, but it should be adapted to the organisation and its environments. The basic steps relevant to all business are:

- analysis of external and internal trends;
- strategic analysis;
- SWOT and issues analysis;
- objective setting;
- strategy selection;
- action plans;
- implementation; and
- performance review and evaluation of performance.

These steps are generally agreed to include the most prominent features of strategic planning. They include, in summary form, the steps proposed by Day, McDonald and Aaker. In practice, the weakest and often most difficult parts of this process are in strategic planning analysis and strategy selection.

STRATEGIC ANALYSIS CONCEPTS

The range of concepts relevant to analysis of competitive marketing strategy emanate from a number of disciplines, including marketing, sociology, economics, financial management and the new area of strategic management.

The product life-cycle

One of the first attempts to form an analytical framework for determining marketing strategy was product life-cycle theory. The product life-cycle concept describes stages in the sales history of a product category or form. Most representations of the life-cycle have the following characteristics:

- A product has a limited life.
- Its sales history follows an 'S' curve until sales eventually decline.
- The inflection points in the sales history locate the stages known as introduction, growth, maturity and decline. Some representations show an additional stage of competitive turbulence or shakeout once the growth rate slows.
- The life of the product may be extended.

- The average profit per unit (of the industry) rises, then falls over the life-cycle.

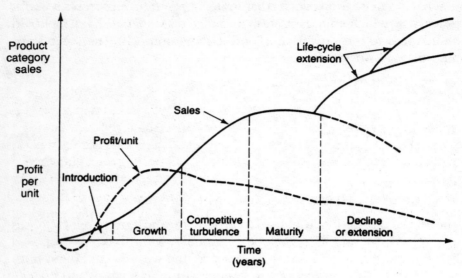

Figure 1.3 Life-cycle of a typical product

Source: Day, G S (1986) *Analysis for Strategic Marketing Decisions,* West Publishing, p 60

Figure 1.3 shows the idealised product life-cycle, which includes curve and unit profit trends.[10] It also shows market extension of the life-cycle. Underlying the life-cycle is the diffusion process and associated adopter categories which are classified according to their timing of entry on to the market. Figure 1.4 indicates the proportion of the total market of each category and the idealised diffusion pattern.

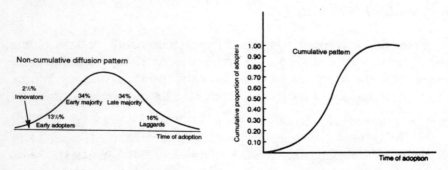

Figure 1.4 Diffusion pattern and adopter categories

Source: Wind Y J (1982) *Product policy: Concepts, Methods and Strategy,* p 28

Innovators represent that 2.5 per cent of the market that will immediately accept the new product and try it. The early adopters are those who will 'make or break' the product depending upon their experiences and opinions. If these are favourable, acceptance grows rapidly and most of the market enters quickly. The last group to accept the product, the laggards, buys for the first time, often when innovators and early adopters have moved to alternative products.

Each stage of the life-cycle represents different marketing challenges. At the introductory stage, the task is to create awareness and achieve acceptance by opinion leaders within the early adopter group. During growth, the challenge is to maintain supply and quality consistency while establishing brand identification and market position. At the mature stage, the firm needs to maintain or improve its profit, defend its position and look for growth segments of the market. In decline, cost reduction, pricing and targeting are important to profitability, and planning is required to determine exit timing. Examples of products at different life-cycle stages in Europe in the early 1990s are shown in Table 1.2

Table 1.2 Products at different life-cycle stages

Introduction	Growth	Maturity	Decline
Filmless cameras	Compact disc players	Microwave ovens	Draught ale
Computer scanners	Facsimile transmission	Washing machines	Typewriters
Stress wave sensing Expert systems	Lap-top computers	Brandy	

Strategic implications

The strategic implications of life-cycle theory are that each stage warrants different objectives, marketing mix, strategies and different management focus. Both Wasson[11] and Day[12] have conducted comprehensive analyses of life-cycle management and propose marketing strategy guidelines for each stage. Each author adds an intermediate stage between growth and maturity, termed 'competitive turbulence', which recognises the implications of the effects of a slowdown in market growth and over-supply, brought on by the entry of new competitors and an increase in capacity by existing ones. Day[13] and Wasson[14] provide a summary of the general strategic implications of life-cycle theory.

An example of this occurred in the British telex market. When it was introduced, telex offered an efficient, quick text transfer service as an alternative to the postal service. It rapidly became an essential business communication tool with maximum market penetration in the early 1980s. British Telecom implemented life-cycle extension strategies by adding features to telex terminals, enhancing user capabilities, allowing text transfer to computers and targeting non-user segments such as small businesses. The rapid growth of facsimile systems since the mid–1980s has brought about the decline of telex and a need for British Telecom to change its strategy to retain profitability and to plan for either product divestment or reformulation to enable future profit to be made on much lower telex volumes.

The introduction, growth and rationalisation of video hire shops is another example of predictable product market evolution. The rapid expansion of retail outlets resulted in over-supply, a shakeout of competitors, and now more stable competition.

Variations on a theme

Life-cycle patterns vary in practice. Some new products skip the introductory stage and grow rapidly from the outset. These are usually products that are readily understood by the market and for which a latent demand exists. Colour television and cellular mobile telephones are examples. New fads exhibit only rapid growth and rapid decline because of a novelty appeal, seasonality and associations with special events. Some products show a decline, then a regrowth pattern. Industrial and consumer durables, such as farm machinery and refrigerators, reveal this cyclical pattern. Other products fail and hardly register a blip on the life-cycle chart. A number of different variations to the life-cycle theme are depicted in Figures 1.5–1.8.[15]

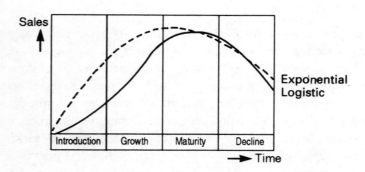

Figure 1.5 Basic product life-cycle stages

Source: Meenaghan, A and Turnbull, P W (1981) *Strategy and Analysis in Product Development,* Vol 15 no 2, MCB Publications, p 2

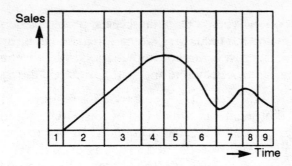

Figure 1.6 Alternative life-cycle shape and stages

Source: Meenaghan, A and Turnbull, P W (1981) op cit, p 2.

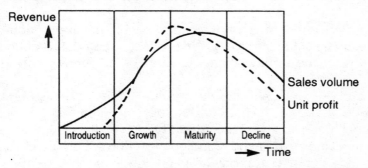

Figure 1.7 Profit-volume relationship over the life-cycle

Source: Meenaghan, A and Turnbull, P W (1981) op cit, p 5.

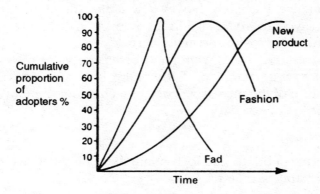

Figure 1.8 Generalised diffusion pattern for a fad, a fashion and a new product

Source: Meenaghan, A and Turnbull, P W (1981) op cit, p 11.

Limitations

The limitations of the concept for developing competitive marketing strategies depend on the variations of life-cycles, problems defining the appropriate market and the focus on strategies that tend to be applicable to the dominant firm in the market and inapplicable to competitors holding different positions. Brownlie and Bart[16] highlight the issues:

- Clear definition of the market is necessary. This requires aggregation of product market segments, which can be misleading where market boundaries cannot be delineated accurately. In practice, it is more common for markets to be defined in terms of several competing brands within a product category. The key question, posed by Weitz and Wensley,[17] is: Which level of aggregation best captures the changing nature of the environment to which marketing strategy must respond?

- As a prescriptive tool, it is too general to enable the application of specific strategy guidelines to a given product or brand. It is difficult to predict when the turning points will occur, based purely on market analysis.

- The concept does not explicitly allow for the influence of uncontrollable external factors such as technology, economic conditions, competitors' position and strategies and the overall capacity of the industry in relation to demand. Conditions of short supply affect sales patterns and can reflect artificial turning points in the sales trends.

- It is not clear how far a firm can influence the shape of the life-cycle by its marketing strategies and at which stages there is potential for greatest influence. It is likely, however, that the pioneering firm and dominant players have a significant impact, particularly at the introduction, early growth and maturity stages.

- The length of stages varies within and between markets. Now, for most product types, duration of the entire life-cycle is becoming shorter because of the increasing pace of technological innovations and introduction of new products.

Practical significance

The life-cycle concept brings into focus a number of market factors that are important for strategic planning:

- The notion of evolution of a market bringing changing market conditions represented by a variety of warning signs is a valuable contribution to marketing strategy formulation.

- Recognition of a finite limit to market potential for a product type sets the market size dimension. Penetration and usage levels at any point provide an indication of future potential.

- The distinction between market sales and a firm's product sales highlights the importance of market share trends and maintaining a focus on the total market. As the market matures, focus on sales trends and cycle stages of individual segments is useful.
- The dynamics of the diffusion process provide useful targeting insights. Target customer groups change over time. It is easier to obtain market share growth during the growth stage of the life-cycle as customers form opinions of brands and try alternatives. As the market matures, customers become more knowledgeable and their perceptions of the product type, and brands within it, change. Distinctions between brands are reduced and the product type becomes 'ordinary', having lost it newness and mystique. Customers progressively develop a 'commodity' view of the product. Figure 1.9 depicts the commodity slide which characterises the maturity of some markets, particularly those in which weaker competitors try to retain profit margins by withdrawing advertising support.
- Identification of products within a firm's range which are in markets at different life-cycle stages provides an indication of the balance of products according to their future growth prospects.
- Recognition of the changing pattern of competition and different types of competitive strategies that may evolve at each stage is a useful contribution to strategic thinking.

The experience curve

The concept

The results of the Boston Consulting Group's ('BCG') studies of cost and price changes in relation to accumulated volume or experience across a variety of industries highlight cost dynamics and their impact on prices, particularly in markets that are growing rapidly.[18] Change in market share can produce change in cost differentials between competitors, enabling a firm which is gaining market share to lower prices faster than its profit margin declines. The per unit cost experience curve, plotted over time in relation to accumulated volume, declines, owing to efficiencies from learning, technological improvements and economies of scale.

Figure 1.10 shows that cost declines with total accumulated volume – this takes the form of a curve on the linear scale. On a log-log scale, it shows a percentage change as a constant distance on the graph; that is, a percentage change in one factor results in a corresponding percentage change in the other. In the case of cost-volume or price-volume slopes, the plotting of data about costs or prices and accumulated experience for

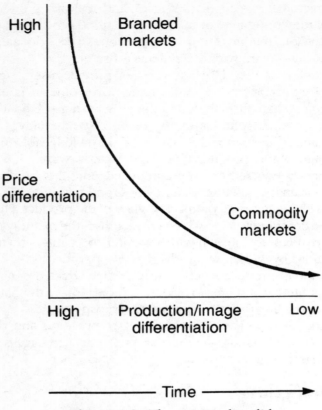

Figure 1.9 The commodity slide

Source: McDonald, M (1989) *How to Prepare Marketing Plans,* Butterworth–Heinemann.

a product on log-log paper in the BCG studies produces straight lines, reflecting a consistent relationship between experience and costs and experience and prices. Across a variety of industries the BCG found that with each doubling of accumulated volume, costs dropped between 20 per cent and 40 per cent, depending upon the industry.

In response to industry cost declines, the BCG found varying price trends – some stable, others unstable. These are shown in Figures 1.11 and 1.12

Strategic implications

Learning experience, and its impact on costs and price levels, has important implications for strategic planning. There is a minimum rate of cost decline required for survival by firms in an industry where learning experience affects costs and prices. This is reflected in Figure 1.13.

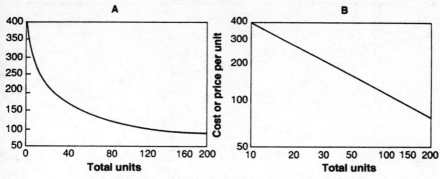

Figure 1.10 Experience cost relationships

Source: The Boston Consulting Group (1970) *Perspective on Experience,* p 13.

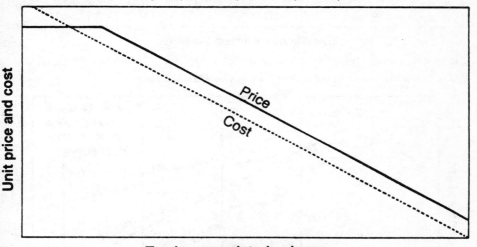

Total accumulated volume

Figure 1.11 A typical stable pattern

Source: The Boston Consulting Group (1970) Perspective on Experience, p 19.

Pricing strategies of leading competitors in a market where learning experience affects costs will create a stable or unstable competitive environment. When a substantial gap develops between average unit price and average unit cost, opportunities exist for lowering prices and gaining more volume. This is usually done by smaller competitors. Figure 1.14 shows this pattern.

The major strategic implication is that firms should seek market share dominance during the growth stage of the life-cycle so that cost advantages can be reflected in price advantages, which, in turn, lead to market share increases. If this is done aggressively, using price penetration strategies it is assumed that the firm will end up with the lowest unit

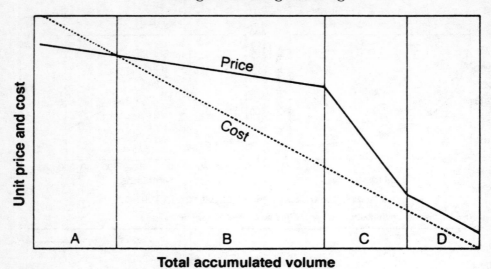

Figure 1.12 A characteristic unstable pattern after it has become stable

Source: The Boston Consulting Group (1970) *Perspective on Experience,* p 21.

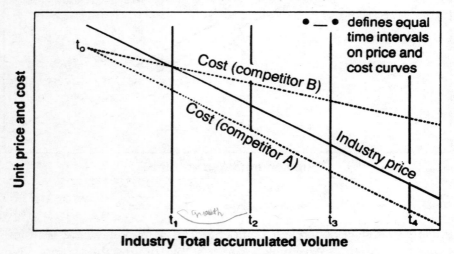

Figure 1.13 Competitor and industry price experience

Source: The Boston Consulting Group (1970) *Perspective on Experience,* p 24.

costs, highest market share and an ability to lead the market during its mature phase. Texas Instruments adopted this strategy in the digital watch market, only to find that its prices ended at a point below its unit costs as the market matured and, despite its dominance, it was unable to make a profit. Clearly, this strategy requires confidence in the fact that volume

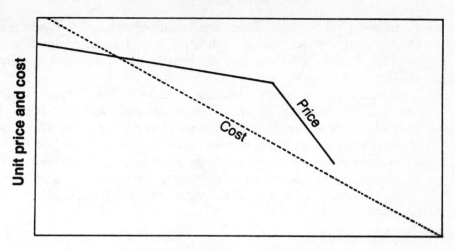

Figure 1.14 Unstable price gap

Source: The Boston Consulting Group (1970) *Perspective on Experience*, p 20.

growth is sufficient to achieve substantial cost reductions and that the firm can achieve, and can sustain, a lowest cost position in the industry.

Limitations of the concept

- The experience curve applies to broad categories of basic products such as television receivers, electric ranges or semi-conductors. When the definition is narrowed into subcategories of these groups, the relationship applies only to the value added component. At the individual product or brand level, this becomes difficult to apply because of the high proportion of joint costs involved.
- Variations in accounting practice can substantially distort reported costs as they affect experience curves and cost-volume analysis. Cost comparisons between competitors are difficult to make for both practical and accessibility reasons. Allocated costs can distort actual product costs. It is difficult, therefore, to gain consistent and reasonably accurate product cost trends.
- An appropriate inflation index is necessary to ensure cost trends are measured in real terms. This is not always readily available for the product type under review.
- Experience can be readily transferred in ways other than accumulated volume. Hiring of experienced staff, licensing of technology, franchising arrangements and acquiring 'experienced' companies in the field of interest, enable firms with low volume experience to operate on a low unit cost structure. Davidow[19] refers to 'toothpaste technology' in high tech industries, where the demands of customers, govern-

ments and industry associations are forcing companies to base their products on identical technologies. More and more products are being built from identical 'product genes' which are now widely available technologies.

Some markets do not respond to massive price cutting because of the nature of the industry. Insurance, furniture removals and medical services are based on trust, and low prices can be perceived in a negative light. Other markets respond to price reductions but, once set in motion, products become low margin commodities with very little profit. Some generic labels sold by supermarkets exhibit these characteristics, where constant price specials are necessary to generate sales.

Practical significance

Despite its appeal and empirical support, the experience curve applies only in certain situations. The earlier broad generalisations have been replaced with applications where the tool is recognised as one of a number of analytical methods. It does, however, focus on some key issues for strategic planning.

Costs require deliberate management to ensure competitiveness as industries, markets and cost structures change. British Leyland found in many of its manufacturing businesses, for example, that it could no longer remain cost competitive, and it divested many of its manufacturing companies during the 1980s.

The competitive marketing strategies adopted by firms in an industry have an impact on industry costs and cost trends. The experience curve concept focuses attention on cost/price/volume dynamics and indicates the importance of forecasting future costs, prices and profits in the industry.

The return on investment from improved market share can be high. The variables affecting profitability are profit margin, market share and market size. In a rapidly growing market, all three are more important in the future than in the present. The strategist needs to determine when to trade profit for future market share and when today's profit is better than more profit on a larger market share.

When experience effects do occur, competitors need to achieve an advantage on those cost elements that are important to particular market segments. These cost elements may differ significantly between segments, allowing specialists to dominate niches against broad line competitors. Davidow, in an account of marketing strategies relevant to high technology industries, illustrates the importance of competitive cost differences and how costs and margin goals affect price.[20] He demonstrates that small differences in costs and margin objectives yield significant differences in prices that can be charged by competitors.

The growth-share portfolio model[21]

The product portfolio concept has its origin in finance theory, where a variety of risk-return investments is balanced as a portfolio to provide the required return to the investor. Some investments are geared to immediate income at a low risk, some to capital growth with low immediate income, and others as higher risk ventures with potentially high future returns. In order to provide for both present and future cash flow, it is desirable to have a balanced portfolio.

When applied to marketing, this concept views products as investments that either require or yield cash according to their position in the portfolio. Some products, especially new ones, will have potentially high future cash flow but are high risk investments. These may require substantial cash investment during development. Others may be declining and represent candidates for deletion. Some products within the range may yield high cash flow, which is used to fund new developments.

Portfolio models, such as the Boston Consulting Group's growth-share matrix, have been almost synonymous with the development of strategic planning concepts. Frequently referred to as the BCG matrix, the growth-share portfolio model classifies each business or product by the rate of present market growth and by a measure of market share dominance. Market growth serves as a proxy for the need for cash, and relative market share is used to reflect profitability and cash generation. Relative market share is the ratio of the product's share to the share of its largest competitor in the same market.

The logic of this model is based on the dynamics of the product life-cycle (market growth rate) and the experience curve effect (the importance of relative market share and dominance). In its simplest form, the model depicts growth and relative share as either low or high. To reflect its future prospects and risks, each product classification is named – star, cash cow, dog and problem child/question mark. The model uses this matrix to suggest market share and investment objectives for each category:

- Stars: invest to hold or increase market share.
- Cash cows: maintain or milk to provide cash for problem child products and research and development.

- Dogs: reformulate to provide positive cash flow, reduce costs, or divest.
- Problem child/question mark: invest in share growth in those that show positive prospects; divest others.

Figure 1.15 indicates the cash flow position of each type and provides measures for placing products in the matrix. The market dominance axis measures the firm's market share relative to that of the largest competitor.

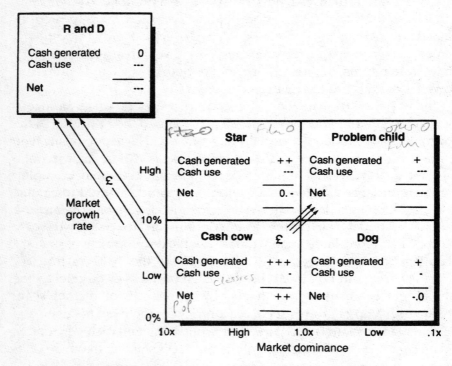

Figure 1.15 Portfolio positions and cash flows

Strategic management guidelines

Brownlie, in a review of the BCG model, provides a useful summary of strategic guidelines.[22] The main guidelines are as follows:

- Star products require continued heavy investment during growth. Low margins may be essential to defer competition and consolidate competitive position.
- Cash cows are managed for cash, but some investment is required to reduce costs and maintain market dominance. Future market pros-

pects will determine how long an investment in maintaining dominance is pursued and when the product is harvested to make the most
profit.
- Problem children are managed to gain market share. Where star
potential is not evident, divestment is recommended.
- Dogs have weak competitive positions in low growth and mature
markets. Most have little potential for share growth and are unprofitable. Liquidation of dog products is usually recommended.

The successful strategy sequence requires the development of a question
mark product to a star, which in turn becomes a cash cow as the market
matures. This may move towards dog status as it is milked for cash, but it
should be withdrawn before negative cash flows occur.

An appropriate balance of cash cows, stars and question marks,
enables the business to produce positive cash flows and profit, while
continuing investment in future profitability.

Limitations

The major weakness of this model is its simplification of complex
situations and the glib guidelines that flow from it. Measurement and
definition problems must be overcome for it to be useful. Narrow
definitions of the market are usually necessary to identify a useful
portfolio of products. An analysis of Unilever's detergent products
undertaken for the detergent market revealed that they were all dogs but,
in effect, they were really golden retrievers, which returned large cash
flows and profit. When the analysis was repeated at the market segment
level, it showed that Unilever had a number of stars and cash cows.

Another limitation is the tendency of this type of analysis to limit vision
and narrow the focus to a range of options that may be inappropriate. The
notion, for example, that 'cows are for milking' does not distinguish
between large share products in mature markets that have long-term
profit and cash flow prospects and require reinvestment and defence of
share position and those that do not have future prospects and should be
harvested for maximum short-term profit and cash.

A further danger is that share may be seen as an end in itself, rather than
as a means to achieving profitability. As Heinz discovered in the 1970s, a
single-minded focus on dominating markets and maximising share does
not necessarily bring with it long-term profitability.

Practical significance

The portfolio concept developed by the BCG does make a practical
contribution to strategic planning, so long as its limitations are realised:

- It is a useful conceptual tool for understanding where products fit in relation to each other in a portfolio and identifying those that require significant investment to improve their market positions. It helps to focus attention on problem products for which management decisions are necessary.
- In common with the product life-cycle, it suggests a competitive evolution of a product from problem child to star to cash cow as the market matures, and it highlights the importance of building market share while the market is growing.
- By drawing attention to cash generation and cash use of products, it emphasises the desirability of a balanced portfolio, so that new initiatives can be funded and cash generators protected.

Attractiveness – competitive position models

The problems posed by the simplified and generic structure of the BCG model are overcome by development of models tailored to the conditions affecting the firm or industry. A number of large corporations use a nine-box matrix to identify the positions of their businesses according to market/industry attractiveness (of which market growth rate in the BCG model is one factor) and business strengths/competitiveness position (of which relative market share is one factor).

General Electric with McKinsey pioneered this model, making use of many variables to assess each dimension. The dimensions used for assessing position are believed to be representative of the significant elements of the internal and external environment from which strengths, weaknesses, opportunities and threats arise. However, the relative importance of these dimensions varies between firms and industries. GE's business assessment matrix, through qualitative analysis, assesses a business as being strong, medium or weak in terms of business strength, and assesses its industry attractiveness as high, medium or low. In common with the BCG model, general strategic guidelines are provided for investment, divestment or selective growth or harvesting strategies.

The Shell Chemical Company developed a similar portfolio model called the directional policy matrix, using as its two main assessment criteria competitive capabilities (similar to GE's business strengths) and prospects for sector profitability (analogous to GE's industry attractiveness).

More recently, a simpler four box version of the directional policy matrix has been developed, together with computer software that enables practising managers to quantify the axes and include circles which accurately represent the relative importance of the contribution to the organisation of the products, services, or markets represented on the matrix.

Strategic implications

These models have the advantage of taking account of specific factors relevant to the industry. Generic strategy guidelines, however, also emanate from them. Figure 1.16 shows a number of strategic options depending upon a business's position in terms of market attractiveness (high, medium or weak). Figure 1.17 indicates directions relevant to four different business positions depending on objectives, resource availability and risk.

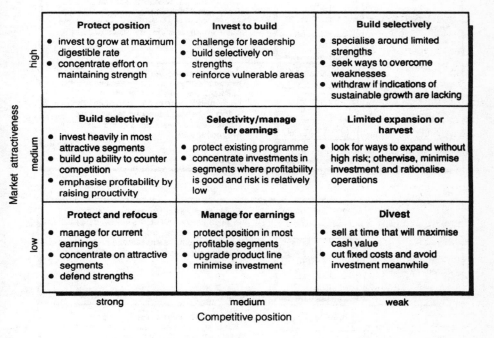

Figure 1.16 Generic strategy options

Source: Day, G S (1986) *Analysis for Strategic Market Decisions*, West Publishing, p 204.

Limitations

The main practical difficulty is the selection and weighting of relevant criteria for assessing a business's position on the matrix. Also, when assessing businesses in different industries, the success factors usually differ, and unless separate calculations are worked out for each, direct comparisons of different businesses on the same matrix may be inappropriate. There are often strategic reasons for staying in a business when the financial indications suggest divestment. For example, Hoover's assessment of the vacuum cleaning market and its array of low-price international competitors, is that manufacturers are prepared to lose money long term in this market because it acts as an entry point to the household for a wide range of appliances and electronic products – the vacuum cleaner being one of the first products bought by new homemakers.

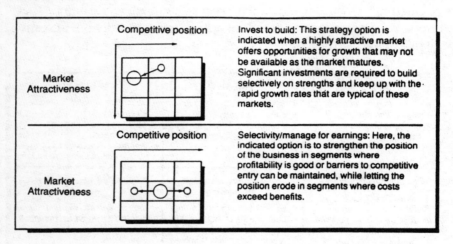

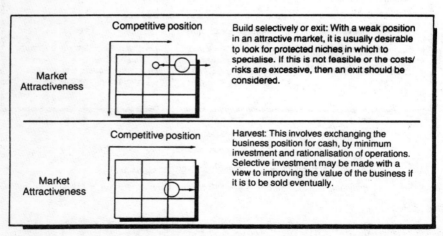

Figure 1.17 Strategy direction

Source: Day, G S (1986) *Analysis for Strategic Market Decisions,* West Publishing, pp 174 and 205.

Practical significance

An important insight from these models is the strategic significance of competitive position as measured by relative business strengths, capabilities and market share. For instance, a market may be very attractive with rapid growth prospects and a wide range of opportunities, but the business's relative competitive position is weak and competitive advantages are difficult to find and risky to implement. Alternatively, the business may have a strong competitive position in an unprofitable, declining market with poor long-term prospects. The implication is that the firm's competitive strength should be used to restructure the industry on a profitable basis or plan to divest from part or all of the business.

Ansoff's product-market growth model

Igor Ansoff, a pioneer in strategic thinking, introduced the concept of the planning gap by first charting expected future sales or return on investment (ROI) based on no change to current strategies, then charting potential sales or ROI based on market potential.[23] In Figure 1.18 two gaps are identified between expected sales from present strategies and maximum sales growth potential – a competitive gap indicating sales potential from the existing business and a diversification gap suggesting sales potential from new businesses. Figure 1.19 modifies this concept to

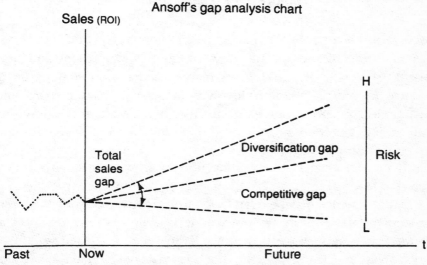

Figure 1.18 Product market directions

show the top-line sales trend to represent management objectives with the task of the marketer to develop strategies to close the gap.

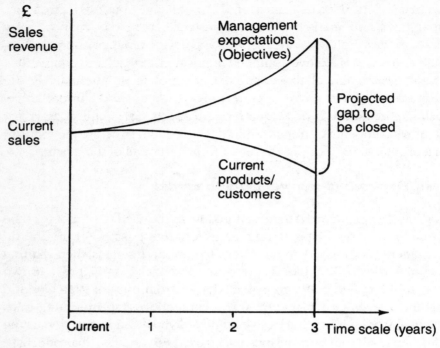

Figure 1.19 Gap analysis

Ansoff proposes options for closing the gap in this growth matrix based on a matching of present and new products with present and new markets, shown in Figure 1.20. A market penetration strategy using products in present markets involves increasing market share and consumption or use from existing customers. Market development requires the targeting of products into new market segments and converting non-users to customers.

Product development enables the firm to grow from new products offered to its existing markets. Diversification requires new products for new markets, which may be related or unrelated to the existing business. The strategic and relevant options will depend upon the size of the gap and the firm's competitive position in its markets. For instance, a high market share in existing markets, such as Asda's position in the north of England, suggests that growth will be sought from new markets such as the south and from new product ranges.

Market \ Product	Present	New
Present	Market penetration	Product development
New	Market development	Diversification

Figure 1.20 Ansoff's growth vector matrix

Source: Brownlie, D T and Bart, C K (1985) *Products and Strategies*, MCB University Press, p 29.

Strategic implications

The product-market growth model has implications for objectives and strategies. Figure 1.21 indicates alternative directions for growth from the established business, where market penetration is the current strategy. Depending upon the firm and its environment, product development, market development or a higher risk move to diversification will be pursued. French and German supermarket groups have expanded into other EC markets as their position in their home markets became saturated. Coca Cola, who for decades followed a policy of market extension, has recently moved along the product development route. British American Tobacco has diversified into a number of growth industries unrelated to the tobacco business.

Brownlie[24] suggests that the sales or profit gap or both can be closed by one or a combination of three major strategies – sales growth, productivity improvement and redeployment of capital resources. Figure 1.22 depicts these options.

Practical application

Although a simplification of the issues involved, the planning gap and product-market growth concepts are a good starting point for identifying the strategic analysis task and providing broad indicators for strategic direction. It can indicate widely different growth or profit expectations from those that are realistic and therefore highlight problems to be addressed by management.

Sometimes, the gap analysis approach will show that the momentum of present strategies will take sales higher than is desirable given the limited supply capabilities of the firm. In general, we find that companies have difficulty meeting demand during the rapid growth stage of the

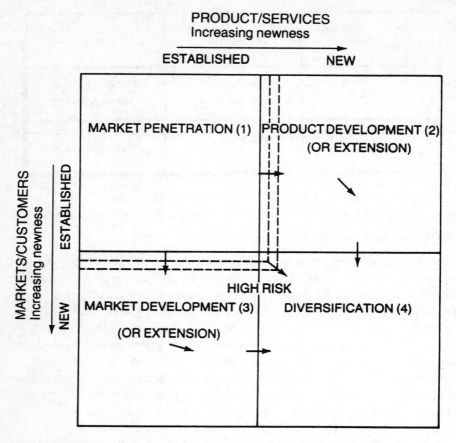

Figure 1.21   Using the Ansoff matrix in the objective setting process

life-cycle. The results of customer complaints, poor service and decline in quality in an effort to meet demand, weaken the firm's competitive position.

The significance of these concepts is that market growth should be managed in line with capabilities to achieve realistic objectives. Strategic planning should, therefore, involve managing opportunities and capabilities to meet objectives. The setting of appropriate objectives is just as important as selecting appropriate strategies.

Strategy experience models – the PIMS model

The basic premise underlying the pooling of business experience is that the conduct of a large series of strategy experiments on companies in a

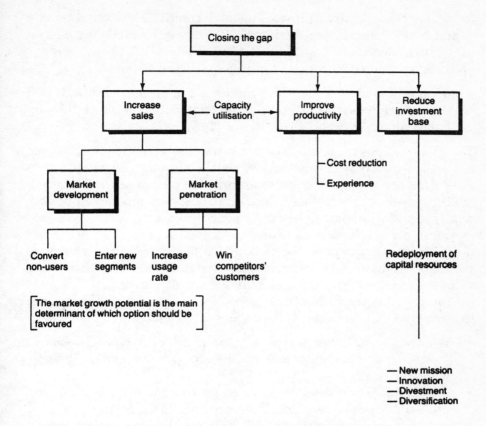

Figure 1.22 Strategy alternatives for closing the gap

Source: Brownlie, DT and Bart, CK (1985) *Products and Strategies*, MCB University Press, p 14.

similar competitive position will provide guidelines on successful and unsuccessful strategies that will be useful in evaluating options under review by a company. Also, the analysis of strategic experience of businesses under different market, competitive and operating conditions, helps to identify the strategic factors that primarily determine profitability. Statistical analysis and computer modelling of the data identify relationships between strategy and performance and provide guidelines for strategic planning. This approach has been adopted by the Strategic Planning Institute in Boston with its PIMS programme, which was initiated in the early 1970s.

The PIMS approach seeks guidance from the collective experience of a diverse sample of successful and unsuccessful businesses. Since 1972 it has compiled a database from more than 450 corporations comprising analysis of over 2800 business units. Statistical analysis and computer modelling of the database provides member companies, which subscribe to and provide information for PIMS, with strategic guidelines based on pooled experience of many different strategic situations in a diverse range of industries. Two concepts are fundamental to the database:

- the business unit – a division, product line or profit centre; and
- the served market – a portion of the total market in which the firm competes.

The PIMS analysis measures changes in the firm's competitive position, the strategies employed to achieve it, and the resulting profitability.

Analysis reveals that three sets of factors are persistently influential in affecting business profitability. One set describes competitive position, which includes market share and relative product quality. A second describes the production structure, including investment intensity and productivity of operations. The third reflects the relative attractiveness of the market growth rate and customer characteristics. Together, these variables account for 65 to 70 per cent of the variability in profitability in the sample. The purpose of the PIMS project is to apply this experience to specific strategic questions. These questions include:

- What rate of cash flow and profit is 'normal' for this type of business, given its market environment, competitive position and the strategy being pursued?
- If the business continues as at present, what market share and profitability performance could be expected in the future?
- How will this performance be affected by a change in the strategy?
- How have other firms in the same industry or in different industries facing the same conditions and similar competitive position performed, given different types of strategies employed?

Answers to these questions can help the strategist to evaluate alternative options under consideration.

The PIMS database is represented by many different industries, products, markets, and geographic regions. Most of these are located in North America, although about 600 of the 2800 businesses are in the UK, Europe and a scattering of other countries.

PIMS findings

This analysis has resulted in observed links between strategy and performance. These general relationships can provide help for managers to understand and predict how strategic choices and market conditions will affect business performance. These are the most common links between strategy and performance:

- In the long run, the most important factor affecting a business unit's performance is the quality of its products and services, relative to those of competitors.
- Market share and profitability are strongly related.
- High investment intensity acts as a powerful drag on profitability.
- Many so-called dog and question mark businesses generate cash, while many cash cows are dry.
- Vertical integration is a profitable strategy for some kinds of businesses, but not for others. For small-share businesses, return on investment is highest when the degree of vertical integration is low. For businesses with above average share positions, return on investment is highest when vertical integration is either low or high.
- Most of the strategic factors that boost return on investment also contribute to the long-term value of the business.[25]

Some selected PIMS findings are shown in Table 1.3. These findings provide some empirical guidelines supporting the use of the market attractiveness-competitive position models reviewed earlier.[26] The cash flow implications of investment intensity (measured by investment as a percentage of sales) and marketing intensity (measured by marketing expenses as a percentage of sales) are given an empirical foundation. The strategic importance of market share and product quality in contributing to profitability is identified.

Table 1.3   Some PIMS findings

Attractiveness of industry – market environment
Market share is most profitable in vertically integrated industries.
R & D spending is most profitable in mature, slow growth markets.
A narrow product range in the early or middle stages of the life-cycle is less profitable than at maturity.
Capacity utilisation is important when investment intensity (investment/value added) is high.
High relative market share (>75%) improves cash flow; high growth (>7%) decreases it.

Competitive position
High relative market share (>62%) and low investment intensity (<80%) generate cash; low share (<26%) and high investment intensity (>120%) results in a net use of cash.
High R & D spending (>37% sales) depresses ROI when market share is low (<26%).

High marketing spending (>11% sales) depresses ROI when market share is low.
High R & D and marketing spending depresses ROI.
A rapid rate of new product introductions in fast growing markets depresses ROI

Capital structure
Low or medium industry growth (<9%) coupled with low investment intensity (<80%) produces cash; high growth (>9%) and high investment intensity (>120%) is a cash drain.
A low level of new product introductions and low investment intensity (<80%) produces cash.
High investment intensity and high marketing intensity (>11% sales) drains cash.
Harvesting when investment intensity is low produces cash.
Building market share when investment intensity is high uses cash.

Source: Brownlie, D T and Bart, C K (1985) *Products and Strategies,* MCB University Press

Limitations of PIMS

Criticisms of PIMS range from definitions of variables, data collection methods and data accuracy, to the non-causal relationships found between variables. Many of these criticisms are valid and should alert the user to treat the findings with care. The PIMS type of analysis can give the user a false sense of accuracy and predictive power. It should be viewed as another source of ideas for strategic planning to be put beside the strategist's own experience, judgement and analysis.

Practical application

The argument that the structure of an industry, the competitive position of the business, its costs/margins/investment structure and the competitive strategies it employs have a fundamental impact on profitability, has strong intuitive appeal.

Practitioners know that a dominant market leader position in a growing market with attractive margins and moderate investment requirements, will bring high profitability. Alternatively, a business ranked third or fourth in competitive position in a mature market with low margins, frequently yields low profitability or losses. PIMS demonstrates that these structural attributes have a significant effect on business profitability and that firms should seek competitive structures and positions that provide them with a profit advantage.

The specific PIMS models and strategic relationships are useful in providing a 'reality test' for the competitive strategies under consideration. They answer questions such as:

- Does this strategy make sense in the light of the experience of others in a similar competitive structure and position?
- Are sufficient resources committed to achieve the desired competitive position and profitability?
- Are the business objectives unrealistic?
- What type of competitive pattern and future competitive structure is likely if this strategy is adopted?

These are important issues to raise, and PIMS analysis helps strategic thinking in these areas.

Industry structure models and competitive strategy

Microeconomic theory focuses on market structure and competitive position as determinants of competitive behaviour. The significance of monopolistic and oligopolistic structures in shaping competitive strategies is recognised by economists in their theories of competition.

Developments by Michael Porter extend this thinking substantially and provide a practical analytical framework for developing competitive strategies involving the structural analysis of industries.[27] He identifies the main structural forces driving industry competitors – industry competition, supplier and customer concentration, availability of substitutes and the threat of entry of new competitors – and suggests that industry profit is affected by these forces.

Porter indicates that the purpose of competitive strategy is to find a position where the company can best defend itself against these forces or influence them in its favour. He studies different industry structures at different stages of evolution and provides guidelines for competitive strategy. Porter goes on to identify the elements of a business that can be used to create and sustain competitive advantage. He considers defensive and offensive strategies for maintaining or improving the firm's market position. This type of analysis is useful in assessing strategic opportunities and competitive threats and is developed in Chapters 2, 3, 4 and 5, where particular application is found in the case studies presented.

In order to influence the structure of an industry or market, it is necessary to identify the important elements of its structure and seek to affect the competitive forces that determine profitability.

The Porter model

Porter[28] suggests that five major forces drive industry competition. These are shown in Figure 1.23. He proposes that the structure of the industry itself, its suppliers and its buyers have a major influence on the evolution of the industry and its profit potential. The threat of substitutes and new entrants also influences the appropriate strategies to be adopted.

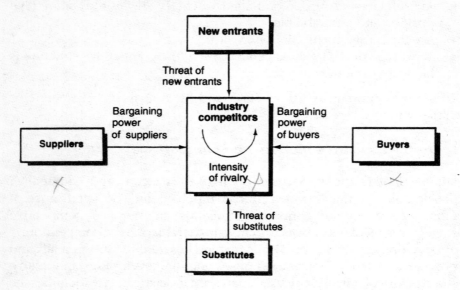

Figure 1.23 The five competitive forces and elements of industry structure

Source: Porter, ME (1980) *Competitive Strategy*, The Free Press, p 4.

The implication is that the competitor should influence the balance of forces through strategic moves, thereby strengthening the firm's position. Alternatively, the strategist might reposition the firm so that its capabilities provide the best defence against the array of competitive forces. A further approach is to anticipate shifts in the factors underlying the forces and respond to them, thus exploiting change by choosing a strategy appropriate to the new competitive balance before competitors recognise it.

A vast range of structural elements may potentially affect these competitive forces. In any particular industry, a small number of factors will be relevant. In the compressed cylinder gas market, for example, the strategic elements for management by BOC, the market leader, are the distribution system, the fragmentation of the customer base and the control of cylinder production and supply.

Evolution of an industry is also affected by the life-cycle stage of its main markets. The large body of life-cycle literature provides marketing strategy guidelines for competitors at each stage. During the growth stage, it is appropriate for market leaders to adopt offensive strategies, whereas in maturity and decline, defensive strategies may be more appropriate. Effective strategies for smaller competitors, however, are different. Where the real opportunities lie for a competitor to restructure the market will depend upon the industry value chain and the contribution of each of the companies at different levels of the supply/distribution/customer system. The value chain concept is elaborated in Chapter 4.

Porter examined industries in different stages of evolution, from emerging product markets to declining ones. Porter considers that in the long term, the extent to which the firm is able to create a defendable position in an industry is a major determinant of the success with which it will out-perform its competitors. He proposes generic strategies by means of which a firm can develop a competitive advantage and create a defendable position:

- Overall cost leadership – aggressive pursuit of an industry-wide lowest cost position relative to competitors.
- Differentiation – development of distinctive abilities that are perceived industry-wide as unique. These may be along several dimensions such as product quality, distribution or after-sales service. In marketing terms, this is known as differentiated marketing.
- Focus – concentrated effort aimed at securing a competitive advantage in a particular market segment or niche. In marketing terms, this is referred to as concentrated marketing.

In terms of product-market evolution, a firm may change its generic strategy over time by moving from a focused strategy to an industry-wide strategy of either cost leadership or differentiation. Alternatively, a firm may adopt a cost leadership strategy, which changes over time to an emphasis on differentiation. Figure 1.24 shows the alternative strategic options and Figure 1.25 the trade-offs that occur between differentiation and productivity gains through cost leadership.

Cost leadership versus differentiation

Cost leadership
Cost leadership is one of two generic strategies in which a firm sets out to become the low cost producer in its industry. Policy choices that tend to have the greatest impact on cost include:

- product configuration, performance and features;
- mix and variety of products offered;
- level of service provided; and
- channels employed (eg, few, more efficient dealers rather than many small ones).

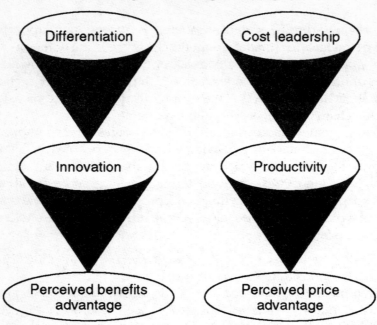

Figure 1.24 Strategic alternatives

The primary focus of the cost leadership strategy is to compete on price as the major marketing tool.

Although the advantage of a cost leadership strategy is that it provides a source of competitive advantage, particularly for market leaders who can use economies of scale, it is usually not appropriate in markets where:

- there is product parity;
- the leader is already heavily committed to an extensive product range; and
- service and channel distribution are critical factors of competitive advantage.

Although cost management and reduction should be pursued where possible, it should not necessarily be the strategic focus for market leaders in declining markets.

Differentiation

In a differentiation strategy, a firm seeks to be unique in its industry along some dimensions that are widely valued by buyers.

In the gases industry, some segments of which are in decline, BOC has selected product availability as the key differentiator and has positioned itself uniquely to meet that need. In similar industries such as auto parts

Differentiation

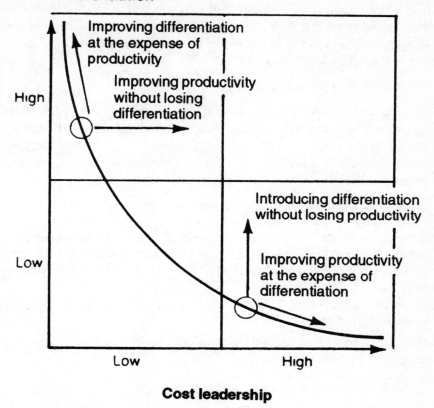

Cost leadership

Figure 1.25 Strategic directions

and accessories, service and distribution are vital differentiators in declining markets.

Product parity usually exists between competitors, and differentiation occurs on availability, service, information provision and price. In adopting a differentiation strategy, a leader will aim for cost parity with its major competitors, but should reduce costs only in areas that do not affect favourably perceived differentiation.

Coverage versus focus

The degree of segmentation of the market and the size of the largest segments, together with the leader's competitive strengths, will determine whether a strategy of coverage or one of focus is required for leadership and dominance of the market. Usually, a leader will need coverage of the main market segments and a strategy may be adopted to attempt to combine some segments with the same product offering. This strategy of counter-segmentation may be viable in declining markets as customers decline to a hard core of users.

Sustainable competitive advantage

The task of competitive strategy is to develop, maintain or defend the firm's competitive position based on a sustainable competitive advantage. The advantage needs to be sustainable because of the considerable investment required to achieve it. Consider the following competitive advantages and their investment requirements:

- the superior product engineering and perception of product quality achieved by Mercedes Benz;
- the brand identity and preference for Coca Cola and Fosters lager;
- the low cost advantage achieved by Aldi Stores and British Telecom;
- the superior knowledge of the fast foods business held by McDonald's restaurants;
- the scale advantages achieved by Cadbury Schweppes in the European market.

These represent elements of sustainable competitive advantage developed by these businesses over many years.

Market structure and competitive position

A firm's competitive position and the market structure in which it operates, acts as a pervasive influence and constraint on its competitive marketing strategies.

Market structure

Most businesses operate in oligopoly market structures defined by a situation in which supply to the market is controlled by a few large producers, the remaining supply being accounted for by small firms. There are a number of substructures of oligopoly, however, which are relevant at the product/market level of competitive strategy. These are:

- monopoly dominance;
- joint dominance (duopoly);
- oligopoly dominance; and
- equal oligopoly.

Monopoly dominance refers to a market structure in which one firm has a very large share of the market (ie share of total industry sales), while all other oligopoly firms each have a much smaller share. In this type of structure, a single firm has such clear share dominance over other firms, that it can, if it so desires, exercise monopoly-like control over both the market and its competitors' strategies. This is particularly evident on price changes. In a market structure of this type, the dominant firm will tend to lead changes in the general level of product prices, with other oligopoly firms following these changes. This is true in the European airline industry, in which the principal national airlines have held a monopoly for decades.

Joint dominance or duopoly refers to a structure in which two companies jointly dominate a market, while all other competitors, as a group, have a small market share. Two types of duopoly dominance occur in practice, one in which the two firms have approximately equal market shares, the other in which one firm has a distinct market share advantage. In both cases, the two dominant firms primarily react to each other's strategies. Either one of the two may be price leader, or it may alternate between them, with other competitors likely to follow changes. The two dominant firms jointly exercise the same types of influences on small competitors, as does the dominant firm operating in a monopoly dominance structure. This type of structure is typified in the UK telecommunications market with British Telecom and Mercury as the principal protagonists.

In oligopoly dominance, the dominant firm has a much smaller share advantage over its next competitor than is evident in a monopoly dominance structure. In such cases, the dominant firm's position is more easily challenged by other oligopolists. Nevertheless, it still remains in a position in which it can lead price changes and limit the flexibility of its competitors, particularly through the use of the price variable. The car rental market exhibits this structure, in which Budget has a clear share lead.

Equal oligopoly refers to a market structure in which no firm has clear dominance. Characteristically, two or more competitors have similar market shares, which are not sufficient to constitute duopoly or joint dominance. In such market structures, price leadership and other forms of competitive behaviour are much less predictable. It is impossible to arrive at valid generalisations on *a priori* grounds. This market structure exists in the European oriented polypropylene market, in which ICI, Courtaulds, Mobil, Moplefan and others, hold roughly equal shares. Likewise, in the European chocolate confectionery market, the leader holds only a marginal lead. The statistics given in Table 1.7 show an oligopolistic situation both in the UK and in Europe overall.

Table 1.4 European chocolate confectionery market share (% by sales volume)

Company	UK	Austria	Belgium	France	Italy	Netherlands	Switzerland	Germany	Total
Mars	24	4	6	11	1	23	9	22	17
Suchard	2	73	82	13	–	–	17	15	13
Rowntree	26	–	3	17	–	13	–	3	11
Ferrero	2	–	5	6	34	–	–	16	10
Cadbury	30	–	–	8	–	–	–	–	9
Nestlé	2	5	3	10	5	–	17	8	9

Source: Henderson Crosthwaite

Meanwhile, the rise of European media outlets such as satellite broadcasting, will change the nature of this and many other markets and a critical mass of product range will be needed to justify distribution costs and to fund new product launches. Also, the large-scale restructuring of the European chocolate confectionery market is expected to drive costs down and to facilitate even heavier promotional spending on brands.

In addition to these oligopoly structures, a fragmented structure, where market share is divided between many competitors, appears in some markets. In the quantity surveying market, no firm holds more than about a 5 per cent market share.

Competitive position

A firm's competitive position, usually measured by its market share, is also an important determinant of the types of strategies it adopts. The Boston Consulting Group recognises this in their product portfolio theory. The BCG growth-share model views products in terms of their market share relative to the largest shareholder in the market – that is, a measure of relative share.

The relevant measure of position is in terms of dominance. A firm may be in one of three possible positions in the market:

1. Individual dominance – in which a firm has a significantly higher market share than that of its closest competitor.
2. Joint dominance – in which a firm and one competitor have approximately equal market shares, which are significantly higher than that of their nearest competitor.
3. Non-dominance – in which the company has a significantly lower share level than one or more dominant competitors in the market.

Its position, identified in these terms, indicates its relative market power and its capability in managing the market, the competition, the direction the market takes and profitability in the market.

Limitations of industry structure analysis

The main limitation of this type of analysis, in common with other models discussed, is that it does not specifically take account of the human and behavioural dimensions of competitive strategy. It assumes that competitors will behave rationally with a profit motive and that they understand the dynamics of the market and competition and the consequences of their own strategies. This is not so in many industries. In the building equipment hire industry, there were many competitors operating on prices below cost at a time when capacity was falling well short of demand. Logic would suggest that prices, margins and profits could all be increased in these conditions – to everyone's benefit in the industry.

Practical significance

Industry structure and competitive position do impose constraints on the range of viable strategies available to any competitor, and their results. Competitive strategies can and do change the structure and position of players in the industry, however, and the objective is to adopt strategies that provide a sustainable advantage to the business within the scope of changing structure and position.

INTEGRATION OF CONCEPTS AND MODELS

Each of the models and analytical tools reviewed in this chapter provides a contribution to strategic formulation. Indeed, there are links between them that provide a more integrated picture of strategic analysis.

Product life-cycle and competitive position

Arthur D Little has linked various competitive positions ranging from dominant to weak with objectives for changing or holding those positions at different stages of the product life-cycle. Table 1.5 summarises these. Brownlie focuses on two competitive positions – market leader (with dominant market share) and market follower. Guidelines are provided for growth, maturity and decline phases, shown in Table 1.6.

Table 1.5 Guidelines for various product life-cycle stages and competitive positions

		Embryonic	*Growing*	*Mature*	*Ageing*
Dominance	⌐	All-out push for share	Hold position	Hold position	Hold position
	└	Hold position	Hold share	Grow with industry	
Strong	⌐	Attempt to improve position	Attempt to improve position	Hold position	Hold position or harvest
	└	All-out push for share	Push for share	Grow with industry	
Favourable	⌐	Selective or all-out push for share	Attempt to improve position	Custodial or maintenance	Harvest
	└	Selectively attempt to improve position	Selective push for share	Find niche and attempt to protect	Phased withdrawal
Tenable	⌐	Selective push for position	Find niche and protect it	Find niche and hang on or phased withdrawal	Phased withdrawal or abandon
Weak	⌐	Up or out	Turnaround or abandon	Turnaround or phased withdrawal	Abandon

Source: Day, GS (1986) *Analysis for Strategic Market Decisions*, West Publishing p 212.

Table 1.6 Competitive position and life-cycle stage

Competitive position	*Growth*	*Product life-cycle stage maturity*	*Decline*
Market leader (dominant market share)	Build market share; reduce prices to discourage competition; develop primary demand and channel strength	Maintain market share; advertise for brand loyalty; product differentiation; price with competitors	Harvest market share; maximise cash flow; reduce product expenditures such as advertising and selling

Competitive position	Growth	Product life-cycle stage maturity	Decline
Market follower	Invest in research and development; advertising and distribution to increase market share; concentrate on a particular market segment; advertise for positioning	Maintain or reduce market share; price to penetrate; reduce costs below the market leaders	No product expenditure; withdraw from the market

Source: Brownlie, DT and Bart, CK (1985) *Products and Strategies*, MCB University Press, p24.

Portfolio, product life-cycle and pims

Table 1.7 indicates the characteristics of strategies suggested by the portfolio approach and their relationship with the product life-cycle.

It is important here not to confuse the stage of the market life-cycle with the stage of the individual product's evolution.

Question mark products may be introduced during any phase of market growth of the product category life-cycle. Cash cows may exist in markets that show significant growth, are static or even declining. Dog products may be declining when various segments of a mature market show growth prospects. The BCG model shows the evolution of a firm's own product from introduction through to maturity.

Table 1.7 Portfolio position and life-cycle stage

Product classification	Life-cycle stage	Product stage	Strategy guideline
Question mark	Growth	Introduction	Investment
Star	Growth	Growth	Maintenance
Cash cow	Maturity	Maturity	Harvesting
Dog	Maturity	Decline	Withdrawal

The PIMS findings tend to support the underlying concepts of growth-share, product life-cycle and the effect of learning experience on costs and profit margins. Figure 1.26 shows some of these findings.

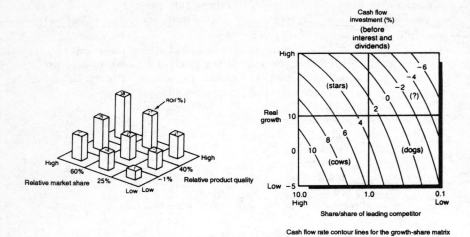

Cash flow rate contour lines for the growth-share matrix

	Market share		
	13%	**27%**	
Early	6	20	33
Middle	11	20	29
Late	15	19	27

(Stage in life-cycle)

Figure 1.26 Portfolio life-cycle and market share

Source: Day, GS (1986) *Analysis for Strategic Market Decisions*, West Publishing, pp 162, 163 and 187.

Strategic position and generic strategies for competitive advantage

Four different strategic positions are shown in Fig. 1.27. These are based on competitive advantage in terms of differentiation or cost leadership and low or high coverage.

Low advantage in cost or differentiation and low market coverage

Here, the business is in a commodity marketing situation, where products are homogeneous, the market structure is fragmented and price competition features. Profit is usually low. It is desirable, if possible, to change this position, unless a cost leadership position can be achieved with resulting market share and profit gains.

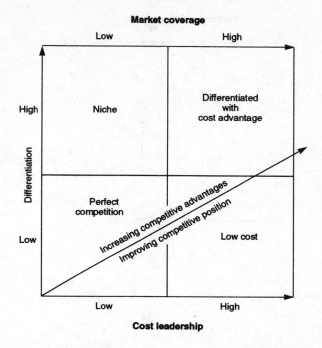

Figure 1.27 Improving competitive position

Cost advantage, low differentiation and high market coverage

This is a desirable position if the cost advantage can be protected and sustained. The volume and market share resulting from a high market coverage should yield profit.

Differentiation advantage, comparative costs and low market coverage

This is a niche position, where emphasis is necessary to protect and improve differentiation. It is viable for small competitors and for large competitors in large volume segments. Share of the overall market is relatively small.

Differentiation and cost advantages with high market coverage

This is the most profitable strategic position, because the market leader has cost, value and volume advantages over its competitors and can command a price premium, with higher margins than its competitors. This position is dominant in market share terms.

For large companies seeking dominance, competitive strategies should be directed at moving towards this strategic position, shown in Figure 1.27. There are, however, different paths from which to choose. The

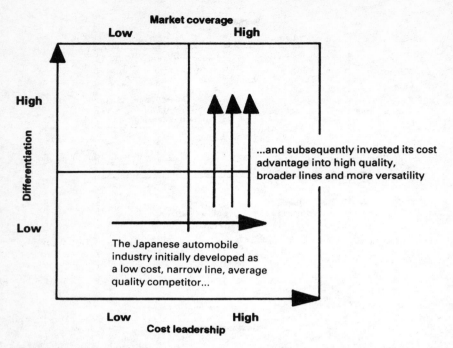

Figure 1.28 The path to competitive position taken by Japanese car manufacturers

Japanese car manufacturers, such as Toyota, have moved from an imitation/commodity position to cost leadership, then to differentiation with cost advantages as shown in Figure 1.28. There is evidence that smaller companies, such as Honda, have now developed niche strategies aimed at competing in specific market segments. McDonald's started as one of many in the fast foods hamburger business, moved to a niche position with product and service superiority, and then to a high volume and market share position, gaining cost advantages while maintaining differentiation (see Figure 1.29).

COMPETITIVE POSITION

A firm's competitive position is fundamental to the selection of competitive marketing strategies. In this book, a broad view is taken of competitive position.

In essence, the factors involved in assessing competitive position are all those which have an impact on market performance, such as sales revenue, share and company/brand image, and on profit performance,

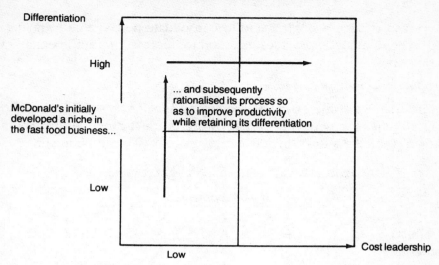

Figure 1.29 The path to competitive position for McDonald's

such as investment levels, costs, margins, prices and productivity and can be evaluated against major competitors.

Assessing competitive position

A number of dimensions are important in practice when assessing competitive position and deciding upon strategies to maintain or change position.

Market positioning

This refers to the relevant market's recognition and perception of a firm's position in the market – what it stands for and what its offerings provide relative to its competitors' offerings. For example, in the computer market, IBM is perceived to be industry leader (the standards setter) and provider of a wide range of high quality, reliable products supported by dependable after-sales service. Companies and their products become positioned in the market's collective mind on a variety of intangible and functional dimensions, which are used by customers to distinguish them.

Market research techniques are now available to identify corporate and product positionings in a firm's target markets. Perceptions of quality, range, availability, image and other relevant dimensions are measured for competing firms. Positioning studies are used to focus a firm's attention on what target customers believe to be important, to improve areas of perceived relative weakness and to consolidate perceived advantages. This type of analysis provides direction to improve or reinforce market positioning.

Product and market coverage

An assessment of the extent of product and market coverage points to opportunities for widening or narrowing product range and segment spread. Table 1.8 shows the relative coverage of two competing firms.

Table 1.8 Product and market coverage

		Market segments				
		1	2	3	4	5
Product	1	A	A	A	A	B
variants	2	A	A	A	A	B
	3	A	A	A	A	B
	4	A	A	A	A	B
	5		A		A	B

Firm A has broad coverage of all except one market segment and has the full range of variants, except in segments one and three. Firm B specialises only in segment five with a full range.

Innovator or follower

The market stance of innovator or follower is determined by the extent and timing of the introduction of new products. Competitors frequently take a deliberate decision on whether to be innovator or follower and structure their research and development functions and marketing departments accordingly. The advantages of being first into a market are well known, but the risks can be high and the costs of failure great. Long-term competitive position is strengthened by a record of successful innovations.

Strategic positions in the market

The market leader has the position of being first in the customer's mind. Kleenex with facial tissues, Hoover with vacuum cleaners, Heinz with baby food, IBM with computers, Budget in rental cars, Xerox with copiers. This, in the long term, is supported by the highest market share.

In some markets, there are two, or even three leaders. This characterises joint leadership. Another position in the market is the high-share flanker, which poses as a serious challenger to the market leader. The remaining positions belong to specialists who focus on market niches.

In many European markets, there is only room for two large

mainstream competitors, a leader and an alternative, and the rest are niche competitors, specialising in narrow segments of the market. Viable positions in the market become strategic because they provide a basis for building, maintaining or successfully defending competitive position. These strategic positions are:

- market leader;
- market challenger;
- market follower; and
- market specialist.

The general characteristics of each viable strategic position are shown in Table 1.9.

The size and structure of the market and the economics of supply will determine how many viable competitors can exist. For example, the British life insurance industry has hundreds of competitors – a market leader, a challenger, about 20 followers and the rest specialists. In the domestic airlines industry, however, there is only a handful of competitors. The market size, structure and characteristics provide opportunities for a range of market positionings based on quality, service, price and image attributes.

The relevance of these strategic positions to competitive marketing strategy is to be able to identify what strategic position a company has, then develop strategies to defend or reinforce that position, or change it.

Table 1.9   Strategic positions in the market

Market leader	
Largest market share	Covers mainstream market
Perceived as industry leader	Maintains share
Leads industry moves	Has the largest profit
	Protects its profit base
	Major impact on the market

Market challenger	
Number 2 or 3 in share	Covers mainstream market
Perceived as an alternative to leader	Increases share
Innovative and aggressive	Investing for future profit
Seeking leadership	Major impact on the market

Market follower	
A significant share	Covers largest segments of the market
Adequate quality lower priced alternative	Holds or increases share
Quick to follow industry moves	Cost advantages
	Limited impact on the market

Market specialist	
Largest share of a small segment	Specialises in a market niche
Small share of overall market	Holds share
Perceived as a specialist	Small, flexible and responsive
	Little impact on the overall market

Market structure and shares

The market structure and shares of individual competitors are important dimensions of competitive position, because they set the scope within which change can take place. Table 1.10 indicates a typical range of structures and share positions found in European markets.

The structure and share positions provide some guidance for formulating competitive marketing strategies. In certain conditions, such as a mature market, the dominant leader in a monopoly dominance structure may want to adopt strategies to defend its share leadership and its overall competitive position.

One of the leaders in a joint dominance structure may adopt a leadership strategy to attain clear-cut market leadership. A niche competitor may want to adopt a growth strategy to strengthen its position in one or two segments of the market or to be a leading force in the market.

Table 1.10   Market structure and share positions

Market structure	Monopoly dominance (1 dominates)	Joint dominance (2 dominate)	Equal oligopoly (3 or more equal share)	Fragmented structure
Market share positions	• Dominant leader (eg 50%)	• 2 leaders in share terms(eg 40%)	• 3 or more substantial shareholders (eg 5%)	• Market share spread between many competitors (eg 5%)
	• Large non-dominant (eg 25%)	• Specialist niche competitors (eg 5%)	• Specialist niche competitors (eg 5%)	
	• Small niche competitors (eg 5%)			

Profitability and resources

This dimension of competitive position is internal to the company, but should be assessed in relation to competitors' profitability and resources. It flags the company's ability or otherwise to fund and continue support for its strategy in relation to competitors.

Internal sources of competitive advantage

Elements such as cost structure, specific skills, responsiveness and other internal characteristics that affect success in the industry, also form another dimension of competitive position. Frequently, as part of a competitive strategy, a business must act on costs or know-how or factors which make the company more market responsive to enable it to improve competitive position. When Lord King joined British Airways as chairman in the early 1980s, for example, he realised that his first priority was to get costs and quality into line before marketing could have any impact on the business.

These dimensions of competitive position have quantitative components (market share, profit, resources) and qualitative ones (market positioning, coverage, responsiveness, know-how). The task of competitive marketing strategy is to improve the quality of competitive position and reduce the risk of disaster. Often, this will require action on many or all of the competitive position dimensions. Although there may be a trade-off between profit and strength of competitive position in the short term, while the firm wants to remain as a strong contender in the market, long-term profitability will be tied to a strong and defendable competitive position.

In most markets, there is room for a market leader, a differentiated number two, a substantial low price positioned competitor, and niche specialists.

COMPETITIVE STRATEGIES

In practice, an almost infinite number of variations in competitive strategy exist, because of the multi-faceted aspects to be dealt with when changing or defending competitive position and the vast array of different market and competitive conditions existing at any point in time.

In considering competitive position from a strategic point of view, however, there are four main directions which competitive strategy can take:

1. developing and building;
2. maintaining and holding;
3. defending; and
4. withdrawing.

The fourth direction, withdrawal, involves harvesting and phased divestment strategies in which marketing's role is to maximise customer goodwill and migrate customers to other products, if that is applicable.

In reality, companies adopt a sequence of strategies that are dependent upon their objectives, competitive position and market and industry conditions. Competitive strategies for building, maintaining and defending competitive position are addressed according to four market positions of firms:

1. dominant position – market leader;
2. position of joint dominance shared with a competitor – joint leaders;
3. a growing force and substantial share – challenger or follower;
4. a growing niche position involving dominance of a narrow segment – market specialist.

REFERENCES

1. Aaker, D A (1984) *Strategic Market Management*, Wiley, Chichester, p 11.
2. Day, G S (1984) *Strategic Market Planning: The Pursuit of Competitive Advantage*, West Publishing, St Paul MN, p 49.
3. Aaker, D A (1984), op cit, p 22.
4. McDonald, M H B (1989) *Marketing Plans: How to Prepare Them, How to Use Them*, Butterworth-Heinemann, Oxford.
5. For example, Porter, M E (1980) *Competitive Strategy: Techniques for Analysing Industries and Competitors*, The Free Press, New York.
6. Kotler, P, Fakey, L and Jatusripitak, S (1986) *The New Competition: Meeting the Marketing Challenge from the Far East*, Prentice-Hall, Englewood Cliffs NJ.
7. Buzzell, R D and Gale, B T (1987) *The PIMS Principles: Linking Strategy to Performance*, The Free Press, New York, pp 6–15, 30–35.
8. Andrews, K (1984) 'Corporate strategy: the essential intangibles', *McKinsey Quarterly*, Autumn.
9. Lubatkin, M and Pitts, M (1985) 'The PIMS and the policy perspective: a rebuttal', *Journal of Business Strategy*, Summer, pp 85–92.
10. Day, G S (1986) *Analysis for Strategic Market Decisions*, West Publishing, St Paul MN, p 60.
11. Wasson, C R (1974) *Dynamic Competitive Strategy and Product Life-Cycles*, Challenge Books.
12. Day, G S (1986) op cit, pp 91–92.
13. Day, G S (1986) op cit, p 90.
14. Wasson, C R (1974), op cit, pp 247–248.

15. Meenaghan, A and Turnbull, P W (1981) *Strategy and Analysis in Product Development, Vol 15, No 5*, MCB Publications.
16. Brownlie, D T and Bart, C K (1985) *Products and Strategies, Vol 11, No 1*, MCB University Press, pp 25–26.
17. Weitz, B A and Wensley, R (1984) *Strategic Marketing: Planning Implementation and Control*, Kent Publishing, p 132.
18. Boston Consulting Group (1970) *Perspective on Experience*, The Boston Consulting Group Inc. Also Day, G S (1986) op cit, pp 25–56.
19. Davidow, W H (1986) *Marketing High Technology: An Insider's View*, The Free Press, New York, p xvi.
20. Davidow, W H (1986) op cit.
21. Day, G S (1986) op cit, Chapter 6 provides an extensive review of the growth-share matrix.
22. Brownlie, D T and Bart, C K (1985) op cit, p 14.
23. Ansoff, H I (1968) *Corporate Strategy*, Pelican Books, Gretna LA, pp 127–131.
24. Brownlie, D T and Bart, C K (1985) op cit, p 14.
25. Buzzell, R D and Gale, B T (1987) op cit, pp 7–15.
26. Buzzell, R D and Gale, B T (1987) op cit, Chapters 5–10.
27. Porter, M E (1980) *Competitive Strategy: Techniques for Analysing Industries and Competitors*, The Free Press, New York, pp 31–33.
28. Porter, M E (1985) *Competitive Advantage: Creating and Sustaining Superior Performance*, The Free Press, New York.

2

Strategic Marketing Planning: What It is and How to Do It

The purpose of this chapter is to remind readers about the key elements of marketing planning and to explain how it can be done. It is in three sections: the first examines marketing planning myths; the second outlines the main steps involved in marketing planning; and the third looks briefly at the implementation and design of marketing planning systems.

MARKETING PLANNING MYTHS

Whatever the precise balance between the many underlying causes for the relative economic decline of nations such as the UK, part of it can be explained by an almost total lack of understanding of marketing on the part of senior managers. However, when it comes to *marketing planning*, the widespread ignorance is devastating. This conclusion is based on a four-year study carried out at Cranfield into how industrial goods companies selling internationally carry out their marketing planning.[1] This survey showed that while all managers agree that it is logical to find some rational way of identifying objectives, to choose one or more of them based on the firm's distinctive competence, and then to schedule and cost out what has to be done to achieve the chosen objectives, 90 per cent of UK companies don't do this. Instead, they complete budgets and forecasts.

What most companies think of as planning systems are little more than forecasting and budgeting systems. These give impetus and direction to tackling the current operational problems of the business, but tend merely to project the current business unchanged into the future. Something often referred to in management literature as 'tunnel vision'.

The successes enjoyed in the past were often the result of the easy marketability of products, and during periods of high economic prosperity there was little pressure on companies to do anything other than solve operational problems as they arose. Careful planning for the future seemed unnecessary. However, most companies today are experiencing difficulties precisely because of this lack of planning and there is a growing realisation that survival and success in the future will come only from patient and meticulous planning and market preparation. This entails making a commitment to the future.

Today, there is widespread awareness of lost market opportunities through unpreparedness and real confusion over what to do about it. It is hard not to conclude, therefore, that there is a strong relationship between these two problems and the systems most widely in use at present – ie, sales forecasting and budgeting systems.

Marketing's contribution to business success in manufacturing, distribution or merchanting activities lies in its commitment to detailed analysis of future opportunities to meet customer needs and a wholly professional approach to selling to well defined market segments those products or services that deliver the sought-after benefits. While prices and discounts are important, as are advertising and promotion, the link with engineering through the product is paramount. But such a commitment and activities must not be mistaken for budgets and forecasts. Those of course we need and we have already got (our accounting colleagues have long since seen to that). Put quite bluntly, the process of marketing planning is concerned with identifying what and to whom sales are going to be made in the longer term to give revenue budgets and sales forecasts any chance of achievement. Furthermore, chances of achievement are a function of how good our intelligence services are; how well suited are our strategies; and how well we are led.

Let us begin with a reminder of some of the basics. Marketing planning is a logical sequence and a series of activities leading to the setting of marketing objectives and the formulation of plans for achieving them. It is a management process. Conceptually, the process is very simple. Marketing planning by means of a planning system is, *per se*, little more than a structured way of identifying a range of options, for the company, of making them explicit in writing, of formulating marketing objectives which are consistent with the company's overall objectives and of scheduling and costing out the specific activities most likely to bring about the achievement of the objectives. It is systemisation of this process which is distinctive and which lies at the heart of the theory of marketing planning.

Naivety about marketing planning

It has long been a source of bemusement that many meticulous marketing planning companies fare badly while the sloppy or inarticulate in marketing terms do well. Is there any real relationship between marketing planning and commercial success and, if so, how does that relationship work its way through?

There are, of course, many studies which identify a number of benefits to be obtained from marketing planning. But there is little explanation for the commercial success of those companies that do not engage in formalised planning. Nor is there much exploration of the circumstances of those commercially unsuccessful companies that also have formalised marketing planning systems.

It is very clear that the simplistic theories do not adequately address the many contextual issues in relation to marketing planning, which may well account for the fact that so few companies actually do it. In fact 90 per cent of companies in the Cranfield study did not, by their own admission, produce anything approximating to an integrated, coordinated and internally consistent plan for their marketing activities. This included a substantial number of companies that had highly formalised procedures for marketing planning. Certainly, few of these companies enjoyed the claimed benefits of formalised marketing planning, which in summary are as follows:

- coordination of the activities of many individuals whose actions are interrelated over time;
- identification of expected developments;
- preparedness to meet changes when they occur;
- minimisation of non-rational responses to the unexpected;
- better communication among executives; and
- minimisation of conflicts among individuals which would result in a subordination of the goals of the company to those of the individual.

Indeed, many companies have a lot of the trappings of sophisticated marketing planning systems but suffer as many dysfunctional consequences as those companies that have only forecasting and budgeting systems.

Operational problems resulting from the forecasting and budgeting approach

The following are the most frequently mentioned operating problems resulting from a reliance on traditional sales forecasting and budgeting procedures in the absence of a marketing planning system:

- lost opportunities for profit;
- meaningless numbers in long-range plans;
- unrealistic objectives;
- lack of actionable market information;
- interfunctional strife;
- management frustration;
- proliferation of products and markets;
- wasted promotional expenditure;
- pricing confusion;
- growing vulnerability to environmental change; and
- loss of control over the business.

It is not difficult to see the connection between all of these problems. However, what is perhaps not apparent from the list is that each of these operational problems is in fact a symptom of a much larger problem which emanates from the way in which the objectives of a firm are set.

The meaningfulness, and hence the eventual effectiveness, of any objective, is heavily dependent on the quality of the information inputs about the business environment. However, objectives also need to be closely related to the firm's particular capabilities in the form of its assets, expertise and reputation that have evolved over a number of years. The objective-setting process of a business, then, is central to its effectiveness. What the Cranfield research demonstrated conclusively is that it is inadequacies in the objective-setting process which lie at the heart of many of the problems of UK companies.

Some kind of appropriate system has to be used to enable meaningful and realistic marketing objectives to be set. A frequent complaint is the preoccupation with short-term thinking and an almost total lack of what has been referred to as 'strategic thinking'. Also, that plans consist largely of numbers, which are difficult to evaluate in any meaningful way because they do not highlight and quantify opportunities, emphasise key issues, show the company's position clearly in its markets, nor delineate the means of achieving the sales forecasts. Sales targets for the sales-force are often inflated in order to motivate them to higher achievement, while the actual budgets themselves are deflated in order to provide a safety net against shortfall. Both act as demotivators and both lead to the frequent use of expressions such as 'ritual', 'the numbers game', 'meaningless horsetrading', and so on. It is easy to see how the problems listed at the start of this section begin to manifest themselves in this sort of environment.

Closely allied to this is the frequent reference to profit as being the only objective necessary to successful business performance. There is in the minds of many business people the assumption that in order to be commercially successful, all that is necessary is for the 'boss' to set profit targets, to decentralise the firm into groups of similar activities and then to make managers accountable for achieving those profits. However, even though most companies in the UK made the making of 'profit' almost their sole objective, many of their industries have gone into decline, and ironically, there has also been a decline in real profitability. There are countless examples of companies pursuing decentralised profit goals that have failed miserably.

Here, it is necessary to focus attention on what so many companies appear to be bad at – ie determining strategies for matching what the firm is good at with properly researched market-centred opportunities, and then scheduling and costing out what has to be done to achieve these objectives. There is little evidence of a deep understanding of what it is that companies can do better than their competitors or of how their distinctive competence can be matched with the needs of certain customer groups. Instead, overall volume increases and minimum rates of return on investment are frequently applied to all products and markets, irrespective of market share, market growth rate, or the longevity of the product life-cycle. Indeed there is a lot of evidence to show that many companies are in trouble today precisely because their decentralised units manage their business only for the current profit and loss account, often at the expense of giving up valuable and hard-earned market share, failing to invest in research and development and running down the current business.

Thus, financial objectives, while being essential measures of the desired performance of a company, are of little practical help, since they say nothing about *how* the results are to be achieved. The same applies to sales forecasts and budgets, which are *not* marketing objectives and strategies. Understanding the real meaning and significance of marketing objectives helps managers to know what information they need to enable them to think through the implications of choosing one or more positions in the market. Finding the right words to describe the logic of marketing objectives and strategies is infinitely more difficult than writing down numbers on a piece of paper and leaving the strategies implicit. This lies at the heart of the problem. For clearly, a number-oriented system will not encourage managers to think in a structured way about strategically relevant market segments, nor will it encourage the collection, analysis and synthesis of actionable market data. And in the absence of such activities within operating units, it is unlikely that headquarters will have much other than intuition and 'feel' to use as a basis for decisions about the management of scarce resources.

How can these problems be overcome?

One of the main difficulties is how to get managers throughout an organisation to think beyond the horizon of the current year's operations. This applies universally to all types and sizes of company. Even chief executives of small companies find difficulty in breaking out of the fetters of the current profit and loss account. The problem, particularly in large companies, is that managers who are evaluated and rewarded on the basis of current operations find difficulty in concerning themselves about the corporate future. This is exacerbated by behavioural issues in the sense that it is safer, and more rewarding personally, for a manager to do what he knows best, which in most cases is to manage his *current* range of products and customers in order to make the *current* year's budget.

Unfortunately, long-range sales forecasting systems do not provide the answer. This kind of extrapolative approach fails to solve the problem of identifying precisely what has to be done today to ensure success in the future. Exactly the same problem exists in both large diversified companies and in small undiversified companies, except that in the former the problem is magnified and multiplied by the complexities of distance, hierarchical levels of management, and diversity of operations. Nevertheless, the problem is fundamentally the same.

Events that affect economic performance in a business come from so many directions, and in so many forms, that it is impossible for any manager to be precise about how they interact in the form of problems to be overcome, and opportunities to be exploited. The best a manager can do is to form a reasoned view about how they have affected the past, and how they will develop in the future, and what action needs to be taken over a period of time to enable the company to prepare itself for the expected changes. The problem is *how* to get managers to formulate their thoughts about these things, for until they have, it is unlikely that any objectives that are set will have much relevance or meaning.

Accordingly, they need some system which will help them to think in a structured way about problem formulation. It is the provision of such a rational framework to help them to make explicit their intuitive economic models of the business that is almost totally lacking from the forecasting and budgeting systems of most companies. It is apparent that in the absence of any such synthesised and simplified views of the business, setting meaningful objectives for the future seems like an insurmountable problem, and this in turn encourages the perpetuation of systems involving merely the extrapolation of numbers. There is also substantial evidence that those companies that provide procedures for this process, however informal, have gone some considerable way to overcoming the problem. Although the possible number of analyses of business situations is infinite, procedural approaches help managers throughout an organisation at least to consider the essential elements of problem definition in a structured way. This applies even to difficult foreign markets, where data and information are hard to come by, and even to markets which are being managed by agents, who find that these structured approaches, properly managed, help *their* businesses as well as those of their principals.

However, there are two further major advantages enjoyed by these companies. Firstly, the level of management frustration is lower and motivation is higher because the system provides a method of reaching agreement on such difficult matters as an assessment of the company's distinctive competence and the nature of the competitive environment. The internecine disputes and frustration which we all experience so often in our business lives is largely the result of an almost total absence of the means of discussing these issues and of reaching agreement on them. If a manager's boss does not understand what his environmental problems are, what his strengths and weaknesses are, nor what he is trying to achieve, and in the absence of any structured procedures and common terminology that can be used and understood by everybody, communications will be bad and the incidence of frustration will be higher.

Secondly, some form of standardised approach which is understood by all considerably improves the ability of headquarters management not only to understand the problems of individual operating units, but also to react to them in a constructive and helpful way. This is because they receive information in a way which enables them to form a meaningful overview of total company activities and this provides a rational basis for resource allocation.

To summarise, a structured approach to situation analysis is necessary, irrespective of the size or complexity of the organisation. Such a system should:

- ensure that comprehensive consideration is given to the definition of strengths and weaknesses and to problems and opportunities;
- ensure that a logical framework is used for the presentation of the key issues arising from this analysis.

Very few companies in the Cranfied study had planning systems which possessed these characteristics. Those that did managed to cope with their environment more effectively than those that did not. They found it easier to set meaningful marketing objectives, were more confident about the future, enjoyed greater control over the business, and reacted less on a piecemeal basis to ongoing events. In short, they suffered less operational problems and were, as a result, more effective organisations.

THE MARKETING PLANNING PROCESS

It is clear, therefore, that marketing planning is essential when we consider the increasingly hostile and complex environment in which companies operate. Hundreds of external and internal factors interact in a bafflingly complex way to affect our ability to achieve profitable sales. Managers of a company have to have some understanding or view about how all these variables interact and managers try to be rational about their business decisions, no matter how important intuition and experience may be.

Most managers accept that some kind of formalised procedure for marketing planning helps reduce the complexity of business operations and adds a dimension of realism to the company's hopes for the future. Because it is so difficult, however, most companies rely only on sales forecasting and budgeting systems. It is far more difficult to formulate marketing objectives and strategies and companies continue to try to make the problem fit somebody else's answer!

The steps

Figure 2.1 illustrates the several stages that have to be gone through in order to arrive at a marketing plan, and highlights the difference between the process of marketing planning and the actual plan itself, which is the output of the process.

A marketing plan should contain:

- A summary of all the principal external factors which affected the company's marketing performance during the previous year, together with a statement of the company's strengths and weaknesses *vis-à-vis* the competition. This is what we call a SWOT (ie strengths, weaknesses, opportunities, threats) analysis.
- Some assumptions about the key determinants of marketing success and failure.
- Overall marketing objectives and strategies.

- Programmes containing details of timing, responsibilities and costs, with sales forecasts and budgets.

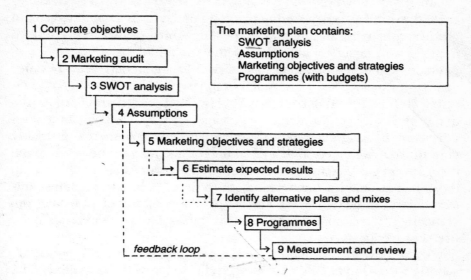

Figure 2.1 The marketing planning process

Each of the stages illustrated in Figure 2.1 will be discussed in more detail later in this chapter. The dotted lines joining up steps 5, 6 and 7 are meant to indicate the reality of the planning process, in that it is likely that each of these steps will have to be gone through more than once before final programmes can be written.

Although research has shown these marketing planning steps to be universally applicable, the degree to which each of the separate steps in the diagram needs to be formalised depends to a large extent on the size and nature of the company. For example an undiversified company generally uses less formalised procedures, because top management tends to have greater functional knowledge and expertise than subordinates and because the lack of diversity of operations enables direct control to be exercised over most of the key determinants of success. Thus, situation reviews, the setting of marketing objectives, and so on, are not always made explicit in writing, although these steps have to be gone through.

In contrast, in a diversified company, it is usually not possible for top management to have greater functional knowledge and expertise than subordinate management, hence the whole planning process tends to be more formalised in order to provide a consistent discipline for those who have to make the decisions throughout the organisation.

Either way, however, there is now a substantial body of evidence to show that formalised marketing planning procedures generally result in greater profitability and stability in the long term and also help to reduce friction and operational difficulties within organisations.

Where marketing planning has failed, it has generally been because companies have placed too much emphasis on the procedures themselves and the resulting paperwork, rather than on generating information useful to and consumable by management. Also, where companies relegate marketing planning to someone called a 'planner' it invariably fails, for the single reason that planning for line management cannot be delegated to a third party. The real role of the 'planner' should be to help those responsible for implementation to plan. Failure to recognise this simple fact can be disastrous. Finally, planning failures often result from companies trying too much, too quickly, and without training staff in the use of procedures.

We can now look at the marketing planning process in more detail, starting with a look at the marketing audit. So far we have looked at the need for marketing planning and outlined a series of steps that have to be gone through in order to arrive at a marketing plan. However, any plan will only be as good as the information on which it is based, and the marketing audit is the means by which information for planning is organised.

What is a marketing audit?

Auditing as a process is usually associated with the financial side of a business and is conducted according to a defined set of accounting standards, which are well documented, easily understood, and which therefore lend themselves readily to the auditing process. The total business process, although more complicated, innovative and relying more on judgement than on a set of rules, is still nevertheless capable of being audited.

An audit is a systematic, critical and unbiased review and appraisal of the environment and of the company's operations. A marketing audit is part of the larger management audit and is concerned with the marketing environment and marketing operations.

Why is there a need for an audit?
Often the need for an audit does not manifest itself until things start to go wrong for a company, such as falling sales and margins, lost market share and so on. At times like these, management often attempts to treat the

wrong symptoms, the most frequent result of which is to reorganise the company! But such measures are unlikely to be effective if there are more fundamental problems which have not been identified. Of course, if the company could survive long enough, it might eventually solve its problems through a process of elimination! Essentially, the argument is that problems have to be properly defined, and the audit is a means of helping to define them.

To summarise, the audit is a structured approach to the collection and analysis of information and data in the complex business environment and an essential prerequisite to problem solving.

The form of the audit

Any company carrying out an audit will be faced with two kinds of variables. First, there are variables over which the company has no direct control: these usually take the form of what can be described as environmental and market variables. Second, there are variables over which the company has complete control: these we can call operational variables. This provides a clue as to how we can structure an audit. That is to say, in two parts: external audit; and internal audit. The external audit is concerned with the uncontrollable variables such as the economy and the markets served by the company, while the internal audit is concerned with the controllable variables, which are usually the firm's internal resources. The panel overleaf contains a checklist of areas that should be investigated as part of the marketing audit. Each one of these headings will need to be examined with a view to building up an information base relevant to the company's performance.

The marketing audit check list

External audit

Business and economic environment

- Economic
- Political/fiscal/legal
- Social/cultural
- Technological
- Intra-company

The Market

- Total market, size, growth and trends (value/volume)
- Market characteristics, developments and trends

  - Products
  - Prices
  - Physical distribution
  - Channels
  - Customers/consumers
  - Communication
  - Industry practices

Competition

- Major competitors
- Size
- Market shares/coverage
- Market standing/reputation
- Production capabilities
- Distribution policies
- Marketing methods
- Extent of diversification
- Personnel issues
- International links
- Profitability
- Key strengths and weaknesses

Internal audit

Marketing operational variables (own company)

- Sales (total, by geographical location, by industrial type, by customer, by product)
- Market shares
- Profit margins/costs
- Marketing information/ research
- Marketing mix variables as follows:

  - Product management
  - Price
  - Distribution
  - Promotion
  - Operations and resources

When should the audit be carried out?

A mistaken belief held by many people is that the marketing audit should be some kind of final attempt to define a company's marketing problem, or at best something done by an independent body from time to time to ensure that a company is on the right lines. However, since marketing is such a complex function, it seems illogical not to carry out a pretty thorough situation analysis at least once a year at the beginning of the planning cycle.

There is much evidence to show that many highly successful companies, as well as using normal information and control procedures and marketing research throughout the year, also start their planning cycle each year with a formal review (through an audit-type process) of everything that has had an important influence on marketing activities. Certainly in many leading consumer goods companies, the annual self-audit approach is a tried and tested discipline integrated into the management process.

Who should carry out the audit?

Occasionally it may be justified to hire outside consultants to carry out a marketing audit to check that a company is getting the most out of its resources. However, it seems an unnecessary expense to have this done every year. The answer, therefore, is to have an audit carried out annually by the company's own line managers on their own areas of responsibility.

Objections to this usually revolve around the problems of time and objectivity. In practice, these problems are overcome by institutionalising procedures in as much detail as possible so that all managers have to conform to a disciplined approach, and secondly by thorough training in the use of the procedures themselves. However, even this will not result in achieving the purpose of an audit unless a rigorous discipline is applied from the highest down to the lowest levels of management involved in the audit. Such a discipline is usually successful in helping managers to avoid the sort of tunnel vision that often results from a lack of critical appraisal.

What happens to the results of the audit?

The only remaining question is what happens to the results of the audit? Some companies consume valuable resources carrying out audits that bring very little by way of actionable results. There is a mistaken belief that a marketing audit is a marketing plan. But, it isn't. It is just a database that has been translated into relevant information. The task remains of turning the marketing audit into intelligence, which is information that is essential for making decisions.

Since the objective of the audit is to indicate what a company's marketing objectives and strategies should be, it follows that it would be helpful if some format could be found for organising the major findings. One useful way of doing this is in the form of a SWOT analysis. This is a summary of the audit under the headings, internal strengths and weaknesses as they relate to external opportunities and threats. This SWOT analysis should, if possible, contain not more than four or five pages of commentary focusing on key factors only. It should highlight internal differential strengths and weaknesses *vis-à-vis* competitors and key external opportunities and threats. A summary of reasons for good or bad performance should be included. It should be interesting to read, contain concise statements, include only relevant and important data, and give emphasis to creative analysis.

Where relevant, the SWOT should contain life-cycles for major product/market segments for which the future share will be predicted using the audit information. Also, major products/markets should be plotted on some kind of portfolio notice to show their desired position over the full planning method. Guidelines on completing the SWOT include:

1. Start with a market overview:

    — has the market declined or grown?
    — how does it break down into segments?
    — what is your share of each?

    Keep it simple; if you do not have the facts, make estimates. Use life-cycles, portfolios, bar charts, pie charts and so on to make it all crystal clear.

2. Now identify the key segments for you, and do a SWOT for each one:

    — list the key factors for success;
    — outline the major outside influences and their impact on each segment;
    — give an assessment of your company's strength and weaknesses *vis-à-vis* competitors. Highlight differential strengths and weaknesses; and
    — give an explanation for good or bad performance.

Assumptions

Having completed the marketing audit and SWOT analysis, assumptions now have to be written.

There are certain key determinants of success in all companies about which assumptions have to be made before the planning process can proceed. It is really a question of standardising the planning environment. For example, it would be no good receiving plans from two product managers, one of whom believed the market was going to increase by 10 per cent, while the other believed the market was going to decline by 10 per cent.

Examples of assumptions might be, 'with respect to the company's industrial climate, it is assumed that:

1. Industrial overcapacity will increase from 105 per cent to 115 per cent as new industrial plants come into operation.
2. Price competition will force price levels down by 10 per cent across the board.
3. A new product in the field of x will be introduced by our major competitor before the end of the second quarter.'

Assumptions should be few in number, and if a plan is possible irrespective of the assumptions made, then the assumptions are unnecessary.

Marketing objectives and strategies

The next step in marketing planning is the writing of marketing objectives and strategies, the key stage in the whole process – if this is not done properly, everything that follows is of little value.

This is an obvious activity to follow on with, since a thorough situation review, particularly in the area of marketing, should enable the company to determine whether it will be able to meet the long-range financial targets with its current range of products in its current markets. Any projected gap can be filled by the various methods of product development or market extension.

We discuss below marketing objectives and strategies in more detail. For now, the important point to make is that this is the time in the planning cycle when a compromise has to be reached between what is wanted by the several functional departments and what is practicable, given all the constraints that any company has. For example, it is no good setting a marketing objective of penetrating a new market if the company does not have the production capacity to cope with the new business and if capital is not available for whatever investment is necessary in additional capacity. At this stage, objectives and strategies will be set for five years, or for whatever the planning horizon is.

An *objective* is what you want to achieve. A *strategy* is how you plan to achieve your objectives. Thus, there can be objectives and strategies at all levels in marketing: for example, advertising objectives and strategies and pricing objectives and strategies. However, the important point to remember about marketing objectives is that they are about products and markets only. Common sense will confirm that it is only by selling something to someone that the company's financial goals can be achieved, and that advertising, pricing, service levels, and so on are the means (or strategies) by which we might succeed in doing this. Thus, pricing objectives, sales promotion objectives, advertising objectives and the like should not be confused with marketing objectives.

Marketing objectives are simply about one or more of the following:

- existing products in existing markets;
- new products for existing markets;
- existing products for new markets; and
- new products for new markets

They should be capable of measurement, otherwise they are not objectives. Directional terms such as 'maximise', 'minimise', 'penetrate', 'increase', etc are only acceptable if quantitative measurement can be attached to them. Measurement should be in terms of sales volume, sterling, market share, percentage penetration of outlets, and so on.

Marketing strategies are the means by which marketing objectives will be achieved and generally are concerned with 'the four Ps', as follows:

- Product: the general policies for product deletions, modifications, additions, design, packaging, etc.
- Price: the general pricing policies to be followed for product groups in market segments.
- Place: the general policies for channels and customer service levels.
- Promotion: the general policies for communicating with customers under the relevant headings, such as advertising, sales-force, sales promotion, public relations, exhibitions, direct mail, etc.

Having completed this major planning task, it is normal at this stage to employ judgement, analogous experience, field tests, and so on, to test out the feasibility of the objectives and strategies in terms of market share, sales, costs, profits, and so on. It is also normally at this stage that alternative plans and mixes are delineated, if necessary.

Programmes

The general marketing strategies are now developed into specific sub-objectives, each supported by more detailed strategy and action statements.

A company organised according to functions might have an advertising plan, a sales promotion plan, a pricing plan, and so on. A product-based company might have a product plan, with objectives, strategies and tactics for price, place and promotion as necessary.

A market or geographically based company might have a market plan, with objectives, strategies and tactics for the four Ps as necessary. Likewise, a company with a few major customers might have a customer plan. Any combination of the above might be suitable, depending on circumstances.

Marketing plans and budgets

A written marketing plan is the backcloth against which operational decisions are taken on an on-going basis. Consequently too much detail should not be attempted. Its major function is to determine where the company is now, where it wants to go to, and how to get there. It lies at the heart of a company's revenue-generating activities and from it flow all other corporate activities, such as the timing of cash flow, the size and character of the labour force, and so on.

The marketing plan should be distributed on a 'need to know' basis only and used as an aid to effective management. It cannot be a substitute for it.

It will be obvious from all of this that the setting of budgets becomes not only much easier, but the resulting budgets are more likely to be realistic and related to what the *whole* company wants to achieve rather than just one functional department.

The problem of designing a dynamic system for budget setting rather than the 'tablets of stone' approach, which is more common, is a major challenge to the marketing and financial directors of all companies. The most satisfactory approach would be for a marketing director to justify all his marketing expenditure from a zero base each year against the tasks he wishes to accomplish. A little thought will confirm that this is exactly the approach recommended in this chapter. If these procedures are followed, a hierarchy of objectives is built up in such a way that every item of budgeted expenditure can be related directly back to the initial corporate financial objectives. For example, if sales promotion is a major means of achieving an objective in a particular market, when sales promotional items appear in the programme, each one has a specific purpose which can be related back to a major objective.

Doing it this way not only ensures that every item of expenditure is fully accounted for as part of a rational, objective and task approach, but also that when changes have to be made during the period to which the plan relates, such changes can be made in such a way that the least damage is caused to the company's long-term objectives.

The incremental marketing expense can be considered to be all costs that are incurred after the product leaves the factory, *other than* costs involved in physical distribution, the costs of which usually represent a discrete subset. There is, of course, no textbook answer to problems relating to questions such as whether packaging should be a marketing or a production expense, and whether some distribution costs could be considered to be marketing costs. For example, insistence on high service levels results in high inventory carrying costs. Only common sense will reveal workable solutions to issues such as these.

Under price, however, any form of discounting that reduces the expected gross income, such as promotional discounts, quantity discounts, overriders and so on, as well as sales commission and unpaid invoices, should be given the most careful attention as incremental marketing expenses. Most obvious incremental marketing expenses will occur, however, under the heading 'promotion' in the form of advertising, sales salaries and expenses, sales promotional expenditure, direct mail costs, and so on.

The important point about the measurable effects of marketing activity is that anticipated levels should be the result of the most careful analysis of what is required to take the company towards its goals, while the most careful attention should be paid to gathering all items of expenditure under appropriate headings. The healthiest way of treating these issues is a zero-based budgeting approach.

MARKETING PLANNING SYSTEMS – DESIGN AND IMPLEMENTATION

In the first section of this chapter we described the widespread confusion between marketing planning and forecasting and budgeting, and the consequences of this, while in the second the main steps in the marketing planning process were outlined. In this final section, some of the *contextual* issues of marketing planning are examined.

The truth is, of course, that the actual process of marketing planning has been described only in outline. Any book will tell us that it consists of: a situation review; assumptions; objectives; strategies; programmes; and measurement and review. What the books do not tell us is that there are a number of contextual issues that have to be considered that make marketing planning one of the most baffling of all management problems. Here are some of those issues:

- When should it be done, how often, by whom, and how?
- Is it different in a large and a small company?
- Is it different in a diversified and an undiversified company?
- Is it different in an international and a domestic company?
- What is the role of the chief executive?
- What is the role of the planning department?
- Should marketing planning be top-down or bottom-up?
- What is the relationship between operational (one year) and strategic (longer term) planning?

A battle against complexity

Many companies currently under siege have recognised the need for a more structured approach to planning their marketing and have opted for the kind of standardised, formalised procedures written about so much in textbooks. These rarely bring any benefits and often bring marketing planning itself into disrepute.

It is quite clear that any attempt at the introduction of formalised marketing planning systems has serious organisational and behavioural implications for any company, as it requires a change in its approach to managing its business. It is also clear that unless a company recognises these implications, and plans to seek ways of coping with them, formalised marketing planning will be ineffective. The Cranfield research showed that the implications are principally as follows: –

- Any closed loop marketing planning system (but especially one that is essentially a forecasting and budgeting system) will lead to dull and ineffective marketing. Therefore, there has to be some mechanism for preventing inertia from setting in as a result of introducing too much bureaucracy into the system.
- Marketing planning undertaken at the functional level of marketing, in the absence of a means of integration with other functional areas of the business at general management level, will be largely ineffective.
- The separation of responsibility for operational and strategic marketing planning will lead to a divergence of the short-term thrust of a business at the operational level from the long-term objectives of the enterprise as a whole. This will encourage a preoccupation with short

term results at operational level, which normally makes the firm less effective in the long term.

- Unless the chief executive understands and takes an active role in marketing planning, it will never be an effective system.
- A period of up to three years is necessary (especially in large firms) for the successful introduction of an effective marketing planning system.

Some indication of the potential complexity of marketing planning can be seen in Figure 2.2. Even in a generalised model such as this, it can be seen that in a large diversified group operating in many foreign markets, a complex combination of product, market and functional plans is possible. For example, what is required at regional level will be different from what is required at headquarters level, while it is clear that the total corporate plan has to be built from the individual building blocks. Furthermore, the function of marketing itself may be further functionalised for the purpose of planning, such as marketing research, advertising, selling, distribution, promotion and so forth, while different customer groups may merit having separate plans drawn up.

A number of points concerning requisite planning levels seem clear. First, in a large diversified group, irrespective of such organisational issues, anything other than a systematic approach approximating to a formalised marketing planning system is unlikely to enable the necessary control to be exercised over the corporate identity. Secondly, unnecessary planning, or over-planning, could easily result from an inadequate or indiscriminate consideration of the real planning needs at the different levels in the hierarchical chain. Thirdly, as size and diversity increase, so the degree of formalisation of the marketing planning process must also increase. This can be simplified in the form of a matrix (Figure 2.3).

The degree of formalisation must increase with the evolving size and diversity of operations. However, while the degree of formalisation will change, the need for an effective marketing planning system does not. The problems that companies suffer, then, are a function of either the degree to which they have a requisite marketing planning system or the degree to which the formalisation of their system grows with the situational complexities attendant upon the size and diversity of operations.

The results of planning

Figure 2.4 explores four key outcomes that marketing planning can evoke. It can be seen that systems I, III and IV – ie where the individual

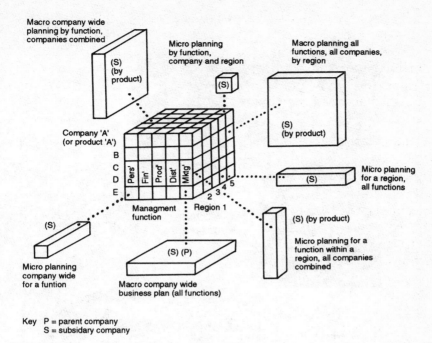

Figure 2.2 Macro business plan: all functions, all companies, all regions, together with constituent building blocks

is totally subordinate to a formalised system, or where individuals are allowed to do what they want without any system, or where there is neither system nor creativity – are less successful than system II, in which the individual is allowed to be entrepreneurial within a total system. System II, then, will be an effective marketing planning system, but one in which the degree of formalisation will be a function of company size and diversity.

Creativity cannot flourish in a closed loop formalised system. There would be little disagreement that in today's abrasive, turbulent and highly competitive environment it is those firms that succeed in extracting entrepreneurial ideas and creative marketing programmes from systems that are necessarily yet acceptably formalised, that will succeed in the long run. Much innovative flair can so easily be stifled by systems. Certainly there is ample evidence of international companies with highly formalised systems that produce stale and repetitive plans, with little changed from year to year, that fail to point up the really key strategic issues as a result. The scandalous waste this implies is largely due to a lack

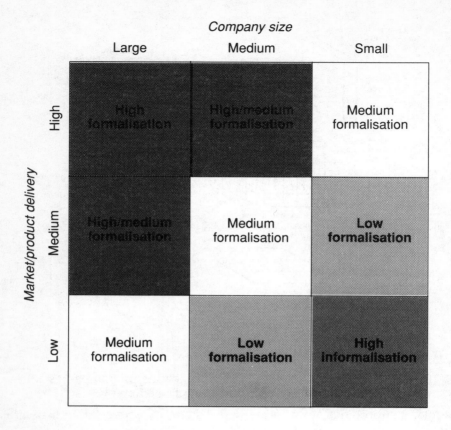

Figure 2.3 Market/product diversity by company size

of personal intervention by key managers during the early stages of the planning cycle.

There is clearly a need, therefore, to find a way of perpetually renewing the planning life-cycle each time around. Inertia must never set in. Without some such valve or means of opening up the loop, inertia quickly produces decay. Such a valve has to be inserted early in the planning cycle during the audit, or situation review stage. In companies with effective marketing planning systems, whether such systems are formalised or informal, the critical intervention of senior managers – from the chief executive down through the hierarchical chain – comes at the audit stage. Essentially what takes place is a personalised presentation of audit findings, together with proposed marketing objectives, strategies and outline budgets for the strategic planning period. These are discussed, amended where necessary, and agreed in various synthesised formats at

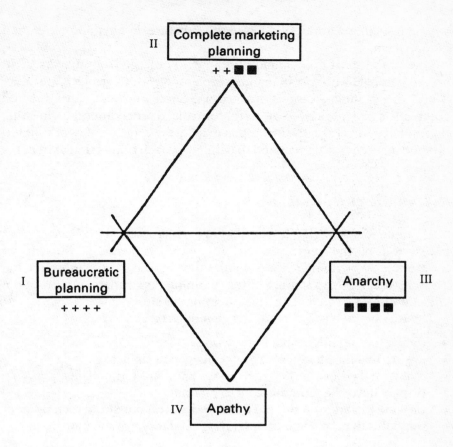

II Complete marketing planning
+ + ■ ■

I Bureaucratic planning
+ + + +

Anarchy III
■ ■ ■ ■

IV Apathy

+ Degree of formalisation
■ Degree of openness

Figure 2.4 Four outcomes of marketing planning

the hierarchical levels in the organisation *before* any detailed operational planning takes place. It is at such meetings that managers are called upon to justify their views, which tends to force them to be more bold and creative than they would have been had they been allowed merely to send in their proposals.

Obviously, however, even here much depends on the degree to which managers take a critical stance, which is likely to be much greater when the chief executive takes an active part in the process. Every hour of time devoted at this stage by the chief executive has a multiplier effect throughout the remainder of the process. And it should be remembered we are not talking about budgets at this juncture, in anything other than outline form.

One of the most encouraging findings to emerge from the Cranfield research is that the theory of marketing planning is universally applicable. While the planning task is less complicated in small, undiversified companies, and there is less need for formalised procedures than in large, diversified companies, the fact is that exactly the same framework should be used in all circumstances and that this approach brings similar benefits to all.

Role of the chief executive

The Cranfield research showed that few chief executives have a clear perception of the purposes and methods of planning, the proper assignment of planning responsibilities throughout the organisation, the proper structures and staffing of the planning department and the talent and skills required in an effective planning department.

The role of the chief executive is generally agreed as being to:

- define the organisational framework;
- ensure that the strategic analysis covers critical factors;
- maintain the balance between short- and long-term results;
- display his or her commitment to planning;
- provide the entrepreneurial dynamic to overcome bureaucracy; and
- build this dynamic into the planning operation (motivation).

In respect of planning, the principal role is to open up the planning loop by means of the chief executive's personal intervention. The main purpose of this is to act as a catalyst for the entrepreneurial dynamic within the organization, which can so easily decay through too much bureaucracy. This is not sufficiently recognised in the literature.

When considering the point in the context of the reasons for failures of marketing planning systems it is clear that, for any system to be effective, the chief executive requires to be conversant with planning techniques and approaches, and to be committed to and take part in the marketing planning process.

Role of the planning department

This role is to:

- provide the planning structure and systems;
- secure rapid data transmission in the form of intelligence;

- act as a catalyst in obtaining inputs from operating divisions;
- forge planning links across organisational divisions – eg R&D and marketing;
- evaluate plans against the chief executive's formulated strategy; and
- monitor the agreed plans.

The planner is a coordinator who sees that the planning is done – not a formulator of goals and strategies.

Marketing planning cycle and horizons

The schedule should call for work on the plan for the next year to begin early enough in the current year to permit adequate time for market research and analysis of key data and market trends. In addition, the plan should provide for the early development of a strategic plan that can be approved or altered in principle.

An important factor in determining the planning cycle is bound to be the degree to which it is practicable to extrapolate from sales and market data, but generally speaking, successful planning companies start the planning cycle formally somewhere between nine and six months from the beginning of the next fiscal year. It is not necessary to be constrained to work within the company's fiscal year: it is quite possible to have a separate marketing planning schedule if that is appropriate, and simply organise the aggregation of results at the time required by the corporate financial controller.

One- and five-year planning periods are by far the most common. Lead time for the initiation of major new product innovations, the length of time necessary to recover capital investment costs, the continuing availability of customers and raw materials, and the size and usefulness of existing plant and buildings are the most frequently mentioned reasons for having a five-year planning horizon. Many companies, however, do not give sufficient thought to what represents a sensible planning horizon for their particular circumstances. A five-year time span is clearly too long for some companies, particularly those with highly versatile machinery operating in volatile fashion-conscious markets. The effect of this is to rob strategic plans of reality. A five-year horizon is often chosen largely because of its universality. Secondly, some small subsidiaries in large conglomerates are often asked to produce strategic plans for seven, ten and sometimes fifteen years ahead, with the result that they tend to become meaningless exercises.

The conclusion to be reached is that there is a natural point of focus into the future beyond which it is pointless to look. This point of focus is a function of the relative size of a company. Small companies, because of their size and the way they are managed, tend to be comparatively flexible in the way in which they can react to environmental turbulence in the short term. Large companies, on the other hand, need a much longer lead time in which to make changes in direction. Consequently, they tend to need to look further into the future and to use formalised systems for this purpose, so that managers throughout the organisation have a common means of communication.

Positioning of marketing planning

There is one other major aspect to be considered. It concerns the requisite location of the marketing planning activity in a company. The answer is simple to give: in the first instance, marketing planning should take place as near to the market-place as possible, but such plans should then be reviewed at high levels within an organisation to see what issues, if any, have been overlooked.

It has been suggested that each manager in the organisation should complete an audit and SWOT analysis on his own area of responsibility. The only way that this can work in practice is by means of a hierary of audits. The principle is simply demonstrated in Figure 2.5. This illustrates the principle of auditing at different levels within an organisation. The marketing audit format will be universally applicable: it is only the detail that varies from level to level and from company to company within the same group.

Because, in anything but the smallest of undiversified companies, it is not possible for top management to set detailed objectives for operating units, it is suggested that at this stage in the planning process, strategic guidelines should be issued. One way of doing this is in the form of a 'strategic planning letter.' Another is by means of a personal briefing by the chief executive at 'kick-off' meetings. As in the case of the audit, these guidelines would proceed from the broad to the specific, and would become more detailed as they progressed through the company towards operating units. These guidelines would be under the headings of 'financial', 'manpower and organisation', 'operations', and of course 'marketing'.

Under marketing, for example, at the highest level in a large group top management may ask for particular attention to be paid to issues such as the technical impact of microprocessors on electro-mechanical component equipment, leadership and innovation strategies, vulnerability to attack from the flood of Japanese and European products, and so on. At

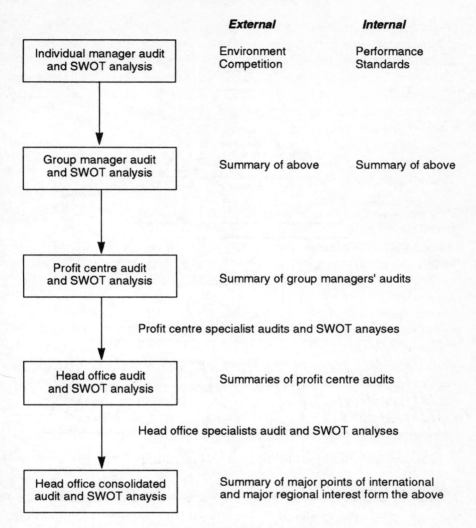

Figure 2.5 A marketing audit hierarchy

operating company level, it is possible to be more explicit about target markets, product development, and the like.

Having carefully explained the point about *requisite* marketing planning, figure 2.6 illustrates the principles by which the process should be implemented in any company. It shows a hierarchy of audits, SWOT analyses, objectives, strategies and programmes.

Figure 2.7 is another way of illustrating the total corporate strategic and planning process. This time, however, a time element is added, and the

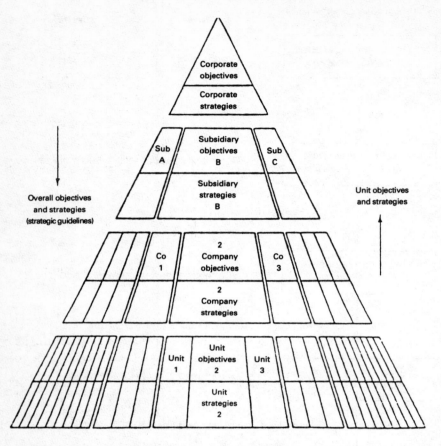

Figure 2.6 Strategic and operational planning – the hierarchy

relationship between strategic planning letters, long-term corporate plans and short-term operational plans is clarified. It is important to note that there are two 'open loop' points on this last diagram. These are the key times in the planning process when a subordinate's views and findings should be subjected to the closest examination by his superior. It is by taking these opportunities that marketing planning can be transformed into the critical and creative process it is supposed to be, rather than the dull, repetitive ritual it so often turns out to be. These figures should be seen as one group of illustrations showing how the marketing planning process fits into the wider context of corporate planning.

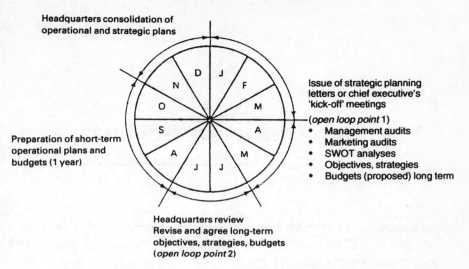

Figure 2.7 Strategic and operational planning – timing

A final thought

In conclusion, it should be stressed that there can be no such thing as an off-the-peg marketing planning system, and anyone who offers one must be viewed with great suspicion.

In the end, marketing planning success comes from an endless willingness to learn and to adapt the system to people and circumstances. It also comes from a deep understanding about the *nature* of marketing planning, which is something that in the final analysis cannot be taught.

The next chapter takes the discussion a stage further. Based on the 1980s Cranfield research, it provides a state-of-the-art review of the latest developments in strategic marketing planning.

REFERENCES

1. McDonald M (1982) 'The Theory and Practice of Marketing Planning for Industrial Products in International Markets', Cranfield Institute of Technology PhD.

3

A State-of-the-art Review*

Strategic marketing demands a perceptive and intelligent analysis of both the company and its business environment. The resulting plan then requires equal proportions of perspiration and inspiration to make it come alive and be brought to fruition.

This state-of-the-art review will focus on two main themes:

1. The development of the 'tools' and techniques available to the strategic marketing planner.
2. The barriers which hamper the introduction of strategic marketing planning, or serve to reduce its effectiveness.

A RECIPE FOR COMMERCIAL SUCCESS?

The claimed benefits of better coordination of interrelated activities, improved environmental awareness, better communication among management, better use of resources, and so on, really are there for the taking, and there is a relationship between marketing planning and commercial success, as the work of McDonald (1984),[1] Thompson (1962),[2] Kollatt et al (1972),[3] Ansoff (1977),[4] Thune and House (1970),[5] Leighton (1966),[6] and others has shown. It is just that the contextual problems surrounding the process of marketing planning are so complex and so little understood, that effective marketing planning rarely happens. What these problems are and how they can be overcome will be dealt with a little later.

---

* This paper is reproduced by kind permission of John Wiley & Sons. It first appeared in 1992 in *Perspectives on Marketing Management*, Volume 2, edited by Michael Baker.

The fact that financial performance at any one point in time is not necessarily a reflection of the adequacy or otherwise of planning procedures (since some companies just happen to be in the right place at the right time, usually in growth industries) should not deflect us from this fundamental truth. Those who question what marketing planning can add in a situation where a company has a well-established position, and where success to date has not been based on any particularly rigorous approach to marketing planning, should remember that all leadership positions are transitory. No industry based in the UK should need reminding of that today. The rapid and systematic demise of the UK's world leadership position is an insult to the founding fathers of British industry.

It is easy to forget the financially-driven management of the 1960s and 1970s who milked dry the results of the endeavours of their entrepreneurial forebears. Rationality to them meant only short-term profits on a product-by-product basis, and if this meant raising the price or deleting the product, who cared as long as the end-of-year profit and loss account came out right? Regard for competitive position, market share, promotion, customer franchise, R&D and the like (all of which, of course, are funded from revenue) seemed irrelevant in those halcyon days of high growth.

Nor should we fool ourselves that this sad state of affairs has changed. A recent study – Wong, Saunders and Doyle, 1988[7] – of Japanese and British companies in the UK concluded that 87 per cent of British firms still have profit maximisation as their major short-term goal, while 80 per cent of their Japanese competitors have market share growth as their major short-term goal. It is a sad reflection on our business schools in the UK that so many of our top industrialists still behave like vandals in the way they manage their marketing assets. It is little wonder that so many of our famous industries and names, such as Woolworth, Dunlop, British Leyland and countless others, have had to suffer the humility of near bankruptcy, and it is a pity that so many more will have to suffer the same fate before we come to our senses and see that marketing planning is crucial to our long-term survival and prosperity.

Whatever the shape or size of the company, marketing's contribution to business success lies in analysing future opportunities to meet well-defined needs. This means that products and services need to provide the sought-after benefits in a superior way to that of competitors.

Let us now turn to the question of the techniques which are available to the marketer, and why it is that they are often neglected, or used in inappropriate ways. To a large extent, this is a reflection of the marketer's understanding of the theory behind the techniques.

DOES MARKETING THEORY HAVE ANY VALUE?

Stephen King's sensitive 1983 paper on applying research to decision-making,[8] focused attention on lack of innovation as one of the key causes of Britain's industrial demise since World War II. His main argument centred on the belief that marketing research in general had failed to address the *real* marketing issues, because so much of it is *quantitative*.

He covered most forms of research in his review, including retail audits, TV ratings, multiple-choice motivational research, conjoint analysis, Fishbein, econometrics and gap analysis, concluding that they can actually be *destructive* to innovation if applied directly to decision-making. I believe part of our national failure to innovate has come through trying to use market research not as an *aid* to decision making, but as a *system* that ideally reduces all personal judgement to a decision as to which of two numbers is the larger.

In a similar vein, Roger Evered (1981)[9] wrote of the emerging realisation that the positivistic science paradigm inherited from the physical sciences has serious shortcomings for the managerial and organisational sciences, and he concluded:

> We must move beyond the objective, analytic, reductionist, number-oriented, optimising and fail-safe approach to future problems, and learn to think with equal fluency in more subjective synthesising, holistic, quantitative, option-increasing ways.

More recently, John Hughes (1988)[10] in his wide-ranging review of the teaching of management education, concluded:

> The mistake we have made in teaching during the past 40 years has been to follow the logic approach to the physical sciences in teaching theory first, followed by an assumed application in practice . . . The bridge from theory to practice is too hard to cross without some prior experience of the 'other side'.

A common theme running through the substantial literature on the growing concern about the appropriateness of the positivistic science paradigm for understanding the process of management, is that much of management deals with judgement, diagnosis and interpretation of events, which requires a different kind of knowing from logic and rationality.

Donald Schon (1984)[11] describes scientific rigour as 'describable, testable, replicable techniques derived from scientific research, based on knowledge that is testable, consensual, cumulative and convergent', but then goes on to argue that much of what passes for scientific management is irrelevant because business problems do not come well formed. Certainly, most marketing problems are messy and indeterminate and successful practitioners make judgements using criteria which are difficult to define. Many academics would decry this as a lack of rigour, and in so doing exclude as non-rigorous much of what successful practitioners actually do.

It is this theme which is of particular relevance to marketing. Moreover, it has less to do with its origin in the positivistic model of science than with the failure of the academic world to understand better what needs to be done to bridge the gap between theory and practice.

The gap between theory and practice

First, however, it is necessary to reiterate that marketing theory is not practised in industry. In no other discipline outside marketing is the gap between theory and practice so great. In 1988, Tony McBurnie, the Director General of The Chartered Institute of Marketing, wrote: 'Research in the early 1980s showed that some two-thirds of British companies did not have clearly defined market strategies and did not use basic marketing disciplines.'[12]

Almost three-quarters of organisations rely principally on extrapolative techniques and financial husbandry. In very few cases is it possible to find any evidence of the use of some of the more substantive techniques taught on most marketing courses, such as the Ansoff matrix, product life-cycle analysis, diffusion of innovation, the Boston matrix, the directional policy matrix, and other strategic and tactical marketing devices.

Nor is this just a European phenomenon. An interesting conclusion from the MSI Expert System Project, ADCAD (Rangaswamy et al, 1988[13]), was that although American companies would actually like to make use of existing theoretical knowledge of marketing, few did.

The most recent study on this topic by Reid and Hinkley (1989)[14] concluded:

> Respondents were asked which techniques they were familiar with. The results were skewed towards ignorance of all the techniques to which they were exposed. The majority were not at all familiar with any by name. The level of awareness of the techniques was not significantly different between Hong Kong and the UK.

The specific techniques which were the focus of the study included BCG, directional policy matrix, Ansoff matrix, PIMS and the experience curve. Similar findings have also emerged from Australia.

There are numerous possible explanations for this lack of usage in industry of the everyday tools of marketing teachers. For example:

- companies have never heard of them;
- companies have heard of them, but do not understand them; or
- companies have heard of them, have tried them and found that they are largely irrelevant.

While all of these (and others) are distinct possibilities, it would be naive not to recognise also that marketing is essentially a *political* process, involving organisational, interpersonal, cultural and social issues which in themselves appear to have no existence as observable entities, since they are contextual and are continuously changing and evolving.

Recent research into marketing and corporate culture (Leppard and McDonald, 1987[15]) goes part of the way in explaining some of the blockages to the implementation of marketing theory as we shall see later. None the less there remains the question of why so many companies that genuinely strive to adopt a marketing orientated approach to doing business still repeatedly fall back on fiscal rather than marketing measures to direct and control the business. In such circumstances, one is left wondering why companies find it so difficult actually to implement what is taught about marketing in business schools.

MARKETING TECHNIQUES, STRUCTURES AND FRAMEWORKS

Most foundation courses in marketing cover at least the following basic frameworks:

- the Ansoff matrix;
- market segmentation;
- product life-cycle analysis;
- portfolio management (Boston box and the directional policy matrix); and
- marketing research and marketing information systems.

Additionally, a host of techniques revolve around the four basic elements of the marketing mix, product, price, promotion and place. Even a cursory glance through Philip Kotler's standard marketing management text[16] reveals a vast and complex armoury of tools and techniques that can be used by marketing practitioners to gain a sustainable competitive advantage for their product or service.

During the past three decades, each one has been the focus of numerous academic and practitioner papers which have sought to explain their complexities and to persuade managers to adopt them as part of the process of marketing management.

Eagerly, devotees of the 'new' message will denounce or drop all the earlier received wisdom as they attempt to force their problems into the latest answer. When the latest fad fails to live up to expectations, it too begins to fade into obscurity, except at management education establishments, where it becomes part of the standard fabric of teaching.

There are, however, a number of problems with this somewhat simplistic explanation of the product life-cycle effect on each of the tools and techniques. These problems revolve firstly around methodological problems associated with the actual tools and techniques themselves, and secondly with the complexity of trying to link a number of them together.

Problems of understanding

If we take a look at some of the more important structures and frameworks used in marketing management, we will observe a number of issues of varying degrees of difficulty in understanding, hence in application.

The product life-cycle is a case in point. There is clearly a difference between a *product* life-cycle and a *brand* life-cycle (Doyle, 1989[17]). It is also pointless for a firm to draw a product life-cycle of one of its own products without also drawing a life-cycle at least of the product class to which it belongs. But the question of how to define the product class (market) to which it belongs is fraught with difficulties. Furthermore, the linkage between the product life-cycle and the diffusion of innovation curve needs to be properly understood. For example, high-priced calculators first diffused through the scientific market, then the professional market, then the business market, then the general market and finally the schoolchildren market. Each bell-shaped diffusion was followed by another, each time adding to the absolute sales curve depicted by the product life cycle, with different cost and strategy implications along the way.

Another well-known, underutilised and misunderstood tool taught by marketing academics is the directional policy matrix (McDonald, 1990[18]). For example, the criteria for the vertical axis (market attractiveness) can only be determined once the population of 'markets' has been specified.

Once determined, those criteria cannot be changed during the exercise. Another common mistake is to misunderstand that unless the exercise is carried out twice – once for $t.0$ and once for $t+3$ – the circles cannot move vertically. Also, the criteria have to change for *every* 'market' assessed on the horizontal axis each time a company's strength in the market is assessed. Some way has also to be found of quantifying the horizontal axis to prevent every market appearing in the left-hand box of the matrix. If we add to this just *some* of the further complexities involved, such as the need to take the square root of the volume or value to determine circle diameter, the need to understand that the term 'attractiveness' has more to do with future potential than with any externally derived criteria, and so on, we begin to understand why practising managers rarely use the device. Indeed, one cannot help wondering whether all the academics have sufficient understanding of the technique to be able to teach it competently. (In order to help readers who would like to know more about the practical implications of using apparently simple techniques such as the directional policy matrix, a more in-depth discussion is provided in an appendix to the chapter, which reproduces the article referred to above.)

Even Michael Porter's apparently more easily assimilated matrix describing the relationship between costs and degree of marketing differentiation has become the latest victim of misunderstanding and abuse through ignorance (Speed, 1989[19]). Reid and Hinkley (1989)[20] drew the following conclusion from their own study: 'It reflects a failure of business schools to disseminate knowledge of strategic methodologies.'

The main problem, however, is not just that virtually every tool and technique of marketing is open to serious misunderstanding and abuse, but that no one method by itself can deliver the kind of benefits demanded by practising managers. Most academics would readily acknowledge the singular contribution to diagnosis that can be made by each device, irrespective of whether it is from the school of life or the more rigorous academic school. For example, while it is easy (and tempting) to dismiss most of what Tom Peters had to say (Peters and Waterman, 1982[21]) largely because of its lack of rigour, few would deny his contribution to marketing by dint of the attention he focused on the importance of servicing the needs of our customers effectively. Likewise, anyone who tries to run their company just on the basis of what Michael Porter says, soon discovers the inherent inadequacies of the nostrum, just as those did who worshipped at the altar of Bruce Henderson and the Boston Consulting Group in the late 1960s and the early 1970s. Yet few would deny the abiding relevance to business in the 1990s of what all these great writers, researchers and teachers had to offer.

To summarise, not only are most of the tools and techniques themselves inherently complex (and therefore misunderstood and misused), but no one tool on its own is adequate in dealing with the complexity of marketing.

Problems of technique interrelationships

There is then, clearly a need to be able to use a number of these tools and techniques in problem-solving, especially when a process as complex as strategic marketing planning is concerned. This raises an additional dimension of complexity for both academics and practising managers, for it then becomes necessary to understand not only the techniques themselves, but the nature of the interrelationships between them, how inputs for one mode can also be used for another and how inputs from some models can also be used as inputs to others.

The problem is that the human mind just isn't capable of dealing adequately with such complexity. This view has gradually emerged as a result of working on a computer-based expert system for strategic marketing planning (McDonald, 1989a[22]) and is confirmed by a number of researchers, including most recently Lock and Hughes (1989).[23] (A more detailed explanation of the expert system – EXMAR – is given in Chapter 5.)

A different approach is required

In the process of constructing the expert system for strategic marketing planning, it became clear that what was needed was some system to link the numerous artifacts of marketing in such a way that outputs from one technique could be used as inputs to other techniques. This was indeed the missing link; as in books and in paper-based marketing planning manuals, the process of marketing planning had of necessity to be iterative, with the onus resting on the user to understand the interrelationships between the techniques used.

The route to this discovery was the data model represented in Figure 3.1. Here, the basic model consists of a strategic business unit ('SBU'), which can be anything from a corporate headquarters to an individual product, is involved in a number of *markets*, and for which it produces a number of products (or services). The system starts with the definition of

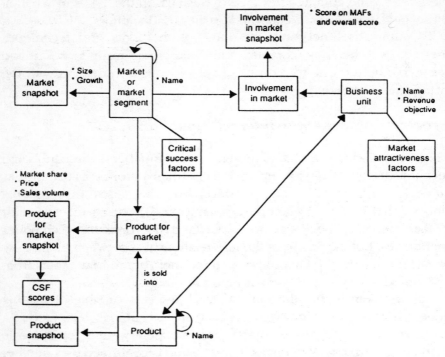

Figure 3.1 Simplified data model in entity-relationship notation

a mission (or purpose) statement for the SBU and indicates very clearly the acceptable structure and the content of such a document.

The next stage in the process was the definition of the contents of a strategic marketing plan and the listing of some of the principal tools and techniques which may be relevant to each of its component parts. It will be seen from Figure 3.2 that some of these techniques may be used for several parts of the plan. However, this does not delineate sufficiently clearly the nature of the technique interrelations, so it was necessary to define in more detail the actual *process* involved in the preparation of a strategic marketing plan.

Figure 3.3 indicates the key steps in the preparation of a strategic marketing plan and some of the subsidiary tasks that have to be completed at each stage. Each one of the boxes on the 'tree' has associated with it a number of marketing tools and techniques, so the next task was to allocate these to each of the main stages in the process.

At the focus stage (Figure 3.4), for example, the output is a statement of those elements of the SBU selected for analysis. In arriving at this focus,

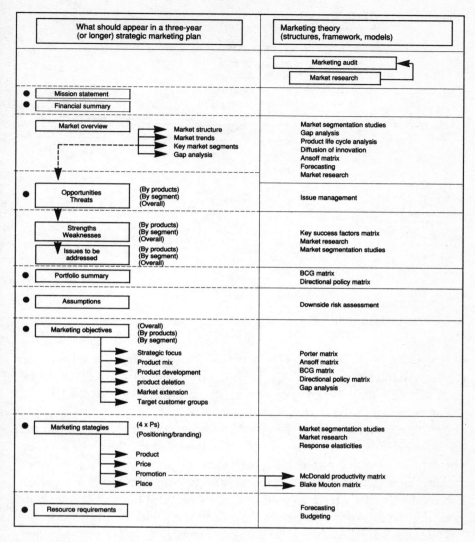

Figure 3.2 Strategic marketing planning and technique relationships

Pareto's law is clearly relevant, as are market segmentation studies (the SIC is provided in the computer system as a possible starting-point for market segmentation). Porter's cost/differentiation matrix may also be useful at this stage if there is a need to have a balance between high volume, low cost markets and more differentiated, niche-type markets. The product life-cycle could clearly be useful in helping decide which markets appear more attractive, as could a knowledge of the cost impact

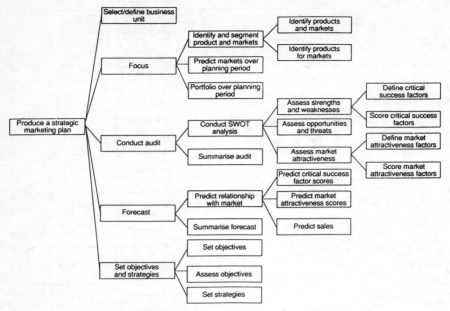

Figure 3.3 Preparing a strategic marketing plan

of experience. The Ansoff matrix is also included here because product/market data associated with each of the four boxes could be useful in indicating the balance between existing and new activities.

The purpose of the audit stage (Figure 3.5) is to complete an in-depth diagnosis or analysis of the selected products and/or markets from the focus stage. Provided here are several checklists to help the program user. The Porter five-force model may, for example, provide useful guidelines at this stage. Detailed instructions on how to construct tables for critical success factors are given, as well as methodological instructions on how to deal quantitatively with external opportunities and threats.

The audit stage has to be summarised (Figure 3.6) and here the Boston matrix and the directional policy matrix can be useful pictorial representations of the current product/market status. Each one of these techniques emphasises different aspects of the same situation. Likewise, gap analysis provides a visualisation in summary form of the revenue and cost implications of current strategies.

It will be seen that the same tools can also be used in the process of setting objectives (Figure 3.7), except that this time they are extended to indicate the desired position at some designated point of time in the future.

Figures 3.8–3.10 indicate relationships between the techniques them-

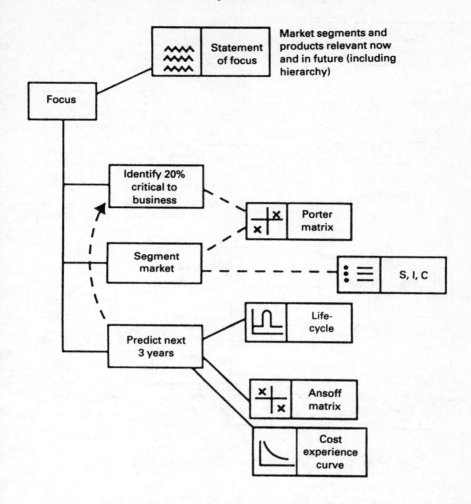

Figure 3.4 The focus stage of plan preparation

selves. Figure 3.8 shows the relationship between some of the principal techniques and their relevance to the basic data model given in Figure 3.1.

Figures 3.9 and 3.10 are attempts to indicate some of the connections between the actual techniques themselves. While it is not necessary to take the reader through every one of these interconnections, it would be useful to highlight at least some of the main ones.

The directional policy matrix can be seen to be a central tool in strategic marketing planning (Figure 3.9). Life-cycle analysis will indicate the prospects in revenue/volume terms for the individual products/markets that are plotted on the vertical axis. The cost/experience curve of

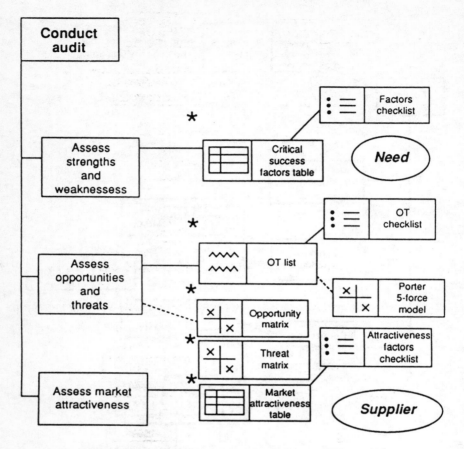

Figure 3.5 The audit stage of plan preparation

individual products/markets will provide valuable input to both the Boston matrix and to the Porter cost/differentiation matrix, which will in turn help in determining the market attractiveness factors and critical success factors which are the basis of the directional policy matrix.

The reader is advised to study these figures very carefully. This advice is given because the expert system manages these interrelationships on the computer and users (typically marketing managers) do not have to concern themselves with them.

On the other hand, if you are either a practising marketing manager or a marketing lecturer, you would be advised to devote some time to thinking firstly about the technical dimensions of the principal tools and techniques of marketing themselves, secondly about their specific applications, and thirdly about the interrelationships between these

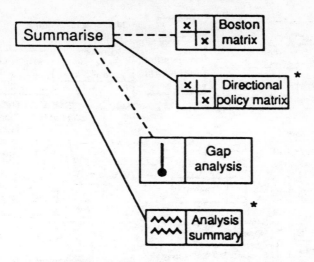

Figure 3.6 Summarising the audit stage

techniques in the process of solving some of the more abiding problems of strategic marketing planning.

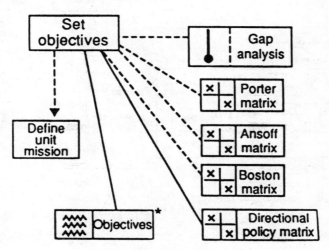

Figure 3.7 Setting objectives

Conclusions regarding marketing techniques

The only reasonable conclusions to reach from the foregoing are:

1. Practising managers must avail themselves of better education in the

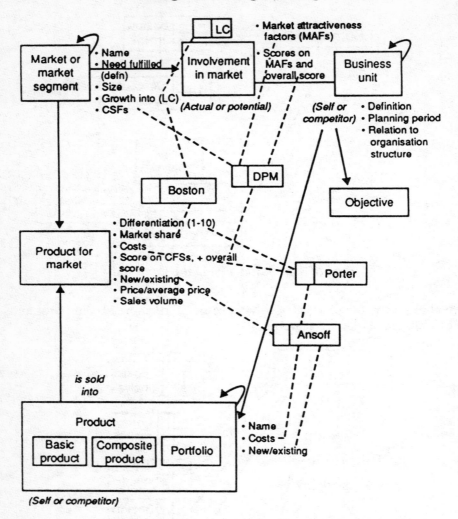

Figure 3.8 Technique interrelationships (I) (showing the data used as input by some of the techniques modelled)

understanding of the application of marketing techniques to real-world problems.

2. There are enough marketing techniques available already, without the need to seek out newer and even more sophisticated approaches.

3. The human mind is largely incapable of understanding and managing the complexities of the relationships between the many techniques of marketing.

4. In view of point 3 above, expert systems will need to be developed so that these complexities are managed by the computer in a way

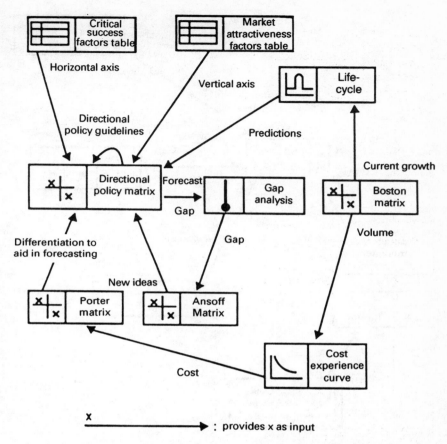

Figure 3.9 Technique interrelationships (II)

which is helpful to practising managers in solving their complex problem.

In this section on marketing techniques, the underlying implication is that if the marketing 'champion' is the 'doctor', whose job is to bring the company back to health, then he would need to know not just about 'medicines' (the techniques), but about the 'patient' (the organisation).

The likelihood of there being a mismatch between the two bodes ill for the patient, yet in reality, that is what often happens. It is easy to see why. All marketing techniques are essentially rational in their construction. In contrast, the organisation, made up as it is of people with all their human qualities and frailties, despite appearances, is often far from being rational.

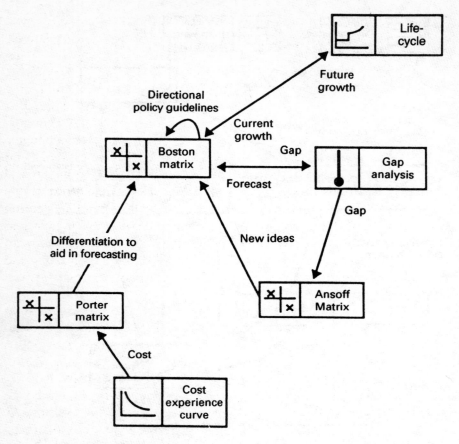

Figure 3.10 Technique interrelationships (III)

The marketer is indeed very much like the physician described by Voltaire: 'He pours potions, about which he knows little, into people, about whom he knows even less.' In reality many of the barriers to marketing planning come from the organisation. It is as if its antibodies fight to prevent the marketing germ from catching hold.

OR~~~~TIONAL BARRIERS TO STRATEGIC MARKETING PLANNING

~r 'short-termism'

companies don't plan where they are going; they do g one step, then look around before taking another.

Sometimes, this journey is in the same direction, sometimes even backwards. Without having a destination to aim for, direction is relatively unimportant.

Nobody will claim that it is easy to identify one's long-term strategic objective, say, three years hence. The task is made extra difficult by the turbulent times in which we live. Yet without doing this, the next one-year step is likely to be irrelevant to the longer-term interests of the company.

It is easy to understand the appeal of short-termism. Most managers prefer to sell the products they find easiest to sell to those customers who offer the least line of resistance. By developing short-term, tactical marketing plans first and then extrapolating them, managers merely succeed in extrapolating their own shortcomings. It is a bit like steering from the wake – OK in calm, clear waters, but not so sensible in busy and choppy waters! Preoccupation with preparing a detailed one-year plan first is typical of those many companies that confuse sales forecasting and budgeting with strategic marketing planning – in our experience the most common mistake of all.

Already, companies led by chief executives with a proactive orientation that stretches beyond the end of the current fiscal year have begun to show results visibly better than the old reactive companies with only a short-term vision. In the old style of company little attention is paid to strategy by any level of management. Lower levels of management do not get involved at all, while the directors spend most of their time on operational/tactical issues. In the proactive case, instead of the strategic orientation just constituting a small part of the chief executive's job, many lower levels of management are also involved in strategy formulation.

The lesson to be learned is simple: develop the strategic marketing plan first. This requires greater emphasis on scanning the external environment, the early identification of forces emanating from it, and developing appropriate strategic responses. All levels of management should be involved in the process.

A strategic plan should cover a period of between three and five years. Only when this has been developed and agreed, should the one-year operational plan be put together. Never write the one-year plan first and extrapolate from it.

Isolating the marketing function from operations

One of the most common causes of the failure of marketing planning is the belief that marketing is something that a marketing person 'does' in their office. The appointment of a marketing supremo is often a last-ditch attempt to put things right when all else has failed. The trouble is, the new person comes along and, irrespective of their knowledge or skills, quickly finds that all the power is vested in others, particularly for product development (the technical people), price (the accountants), customer service (the distribution department) and selling (the sales director). This leaves some bits of the promotional mix for the new person to play around with. Hence the new executive is powerless to influence anything of significance and quickly fails.

Line managers look on the new department with disdain and see requests for information, strategies and plans as a time-consuming task likely to have little impact on their real and more pressing problems.

This has much to do with the general misunderstanding about what marketing really is. Without a corporate driving force centred around customer satisfaction (ie a marketing orientation), arguments about where to put marketing are of course pointless, but even when top management is jolted into a realisation of the need to take account of the customer, the most frequent mistake is to separate out marketing from operations.

This is not the place to argue about organisational issues, such as line versus staff, centralisation versus decentralisation, although the principles are clear: for the purpose of marketing planning, put marketing as close as possible to the customer. Where practicable, have both marketing and sales report to the same person, who should not normally be the chief executive officer.

Confusion between the marketing function and the marketing concept

The author's close contact with about 2000 senior managers a year confirms his belief about the depth of ignorance that still abounds concerning what marketing is:

1. Confusion with sales. One managing director aggressively announced to the assembled seminar audience, 'There's no time for marketing in my company 'til sales improve!' Confusion with sales is still one of the biggest barriers to overcome.
2. Confusion with product management. The belief that all a company has to do is to produce a good product to succeed also still abounds, and neither Concorde, the EMI body-scanner, nor the many thousands of brilliant British products that have seen their owners or inventors go bankrupt, will convince such people otherwise.
3. Confusion with advertising. This is another popular misconception

and the annals of business are replete with examples such as Dunlop, Woolworth and British Airways who, before getting professional advertising management in, won awards with their 'brilliant' campaigns, while failing to deliver the goods. Throwing advertising expenditure at them is still a very popular way of tackling deep-rooted marketing problems.

4. Confusion with customer service. The 'have a nice day' syndrome is currently having its heyday in many countries of the world, popularised of course by Peters and Waterman in *In Search of Excellence*. The banks are among those who have spent millions training their staff to be charming to customers while still getting the basic offer fundamentally wrong – the banks are still closed when the public most needs them open. Likewise, in British Rail, while it helps to be treated nicely, it is actually much more important for passengers to arrive on time.

The principle, then, is as follows: marketing is a management process whereby the resources of the whole organisation are utilised to satisfy the needs of selected customer groups in order to achieve the objectives of both parties. Marketing, then, is first and foremost an attitude of mind rather than a series of functional activities.

Structural barriers

Closely linked with the issues of marketing powerlessness is the issue of organisational form or structure.

The most typical organigram is the one which is based around corporate functions such as personnel, finance, production, distribution, operations and marketing. While the traditional reasons for this type of organisation are clear, there is little doubt that it can be very difficult to get people who are loyal to their own 'tribe' to think of subjugating their own goals to the broader goals of customer satisfaction. This is clearly the role of top management and has a lot to do with corporate culture, to be discussed below.

While the team building approach has gone a long way towards overcoming this kind of organisational barrier, of much more importance is to get the task of defining strategic business units right (Strategic Planning Institute, 1986[24]). A strategic business unit:

- will have common segments and competitors for most of its products;
- is a competitor in an external market;
- is a discrete, separable and identifiable unit; and

- will have a manager who has control over most of the areas critical to success.

But SBUs are not necessarily the same as operating units, and the definition can, and should, be applied all the way down to a particular product or customer or group of products or customers, and it is here that the main marketing planning task lies. The problem remains of getting organisational support and commitment to the marketing planning process, but this is discussed later.

Organise company activities around customer groups if possible rather than around functional activities and get marketing planning done in these strategic business units. Without excellent marketing planning in SBUs, corporate marketing planning will be of limited value.

Lack of in-depth analysis

Even from well-respected companies, the most common complaint concerns lack of adequate information for the purpose of analysis. On deeper investigation, however, it nearly always turns out to be a case of too much information rather than too little. The real problem is frequently lack of proper analysis. At a recent conference there was a builders merchant company that had increased its net profit before tax by 60 per cent for the second year running, but their chief executives did not know the answer to any of the following questions. How much of the profit increase is due to:

- market size growth?
- market share growth?
- price increases?
- cost reductions?
- productivity improvements?

Faced with such massive ignorance, it is clear what will happen to this company the moment construction industry trading conditions worsen.

The methodology for developing marketing intelligence systems has been comprehensively covered in the literature during the past 20 years, yet it is clear that in Britain at least, industry has a long way to go to get even the basics right concerning trends in:

- the environment;
- markets;
- competitors; and
- internal strengths and weaknesses.

It is also clear that, even if an organisation has an adequate intelligence system, rarely is there a formal marketing audit undertaken by all SBU managers as a required activity at a specific time of the year as part of an agreed planning process.

The principle, then, is as follows – for an effective marketing audit to take place:

- checklists of questions customised according to level in the organisation should be agreed;
- these should form the basis of the organisation's MIS;
- the marketing audit should be a required activity;
- managers should not be allowed to hide behind vague terms like 'poor economic conditions'; and
- managers should be encouraged to incorporate the tools of marketing in their audits – eg product life-cycles, product portfolios, and the like.

Confusion between process and output

Confusion between the management process itself and the output of the process, the marketing plan, is common. In most cases, plans are too bulky to be of any practical use to busy line managers and most contain masses of data and information which rightly belong in the company's marketing information system or audit, and inclusion of which in the marketing plan only serves to rob it of focus and impact.

The SWOT device (strengths, weaknesses, opportunities and threats), while potentially a very powerful analytical device to give impact to the ensuing assumptions, objectives, strategies and budgets, is rarely used effectively. A SWOT should:

- be focused on each specific segment of crucial importance to the organisation's future;
- be a summary emanating from the marketing audit;
- be brief, interesting and concise;
- focus on key factors only;
- list differential strengths and weakness *vis-à-vis* competitors, focusing on competitive advantage;
- list key external opportunities and threats only;
- identify and pin down the real issues – it should not be a list of unrelated points;
- enable the reader to grasp instantly the main thrust of the business, even to the point of being able to write marketing objectives; and

- answer the implied questions 'which means that ...?' to get the real implications.

This leads to a key point which needs to be made about this vital part of the marketing planning process: information is the foundation on which a marketing plan is built. From information (internal and external) comes intelligence. Intelligence describes the marketing plan, which is the intellectualisation of how managers perceive their own position in their markets relative to their competitors (with competitive advantage accurately defined – eg cost leader, differentiation, niche), what objectives they want to achieve over some designated period of time, how they intend to achieve their objectives (strategies), what resources are required, and with what results (budget).

Lack of knowledge and skills

As we have seen, it is a matter of great disappointment to academics that many of the components of a typical marketing syllabus are rarely used by practising marketing managers, at least in industrial goods organisations. Indeed, in the author's experience, even experienced marketing managers with marketing qualifications often fail to apply the techniques of marketing in their jobs.

The perennial problems have always centred on customer behaviour and market segmentation, and indeed these are extremely difficult concepts to grasp even at the cognitive level. Even more worrying, however, is the blind assumption often made by top management that all the key marketing practitioners in an organisation actually possess both the knowledge and the skills to be effective marketers.

The author has conducted a series of experiments in some of the UK's leading companies during the past two years, and has found that almost two-thirds of marketing practitioners do not know the difference between a corporate objective, a marketing objective, and an advertising objective. Even fewer know what a logarithmic scale is and how it can be used in experience curves and matrices. Very few have heard of the Standard Industrial Classification and virtually no one has heard of PIMS. Very few even understand the significance of benefit analysis, let alone benefit segmentation. Out of 50 questions, the average score is about 20 per cent.

While these are only examples, and do not prove anything, it must be a matter of concern when thinking seriously about marketing planning, for without an understanding of at least some of the basic tools of marketing, the chance of coming up with strategies based on sustainable competitive advantage is slim.

Communication and interpersonal skills are also prerequisites for marketing planning success, since excellent marketing plans will be ineffective unless those on whom the main burden of implementation lies understand them and are highly motivated towards their achievement. The principle then is to ensure all those responsible for marketing in SBUs have the necessary marketing knowledge and skills for the job. In particular, ensure they understand and know how to use the more important tools of marketing, such as:

- information
  - how to get it
  - how to use it
- positioning
  - market segmentation
  - Ansoff
  - Porter
- product life-cycle analysis
  - gap analysis
- portfolio management
  - BCG
  - directional policy matrix
- 4Ps management
  - product
  - price
  - place
  - promotion

Additionally, marketing personnel require communication and interpersonal skills.

Lack of a systematic approach to marketing planning

Gorb (1978)[25] talks about the differences between a hunter and a farmer in planning requirements. A hunter travels light, and needs stealth, cunning and know-how, whereas a farmer needs to plan ahead, buy seed, sow, harvest, interpret demand for the crops, and so on. Clearly, then, at the entrepreneurial end of corporate development, marketing planning as a formalised system is not likely to be seen as relevant because of the 'here and now' ethos.

Leppard (1987)[26] discusses the different kinds of planning system that are required by organisations. These range from very informal systems to highly formalised ones, with the degree of autonomy at the top or bottom depending on the organisation's size and stage of development. He also devised an analytical tool for measuring an organisation's stage of development to ensure that any marketing planning system is appropriate.

The point here, however, is that for all but very small, undiversified organisations, a marketing planning system is essential to ensure that things happen when they are supposed to happen and that there are at least some basic standards which must be adhered to. In the author's experience even where training has been carried out, the quality and usefulness of SBU marketing plans are so variable as to make headquarters coordination into a central document an impossible task. This is largely due to the different levels of intellect and motivation of participating managers. It is essential to have a set of written procedures and a well-argued common format for marketing planning. The purposes of such a system are:

- to ensure all key issues are systematically considered;
- to pull together the essential elements of the strategic planning of each SBU in a consistent manner; and
- to help corporate management to compare diverse businesses and to understand the overall condition of and prospects for the organisation.

Failure to prioritise objectives

Even when organisations are successful in producing well-reasoned marketing plans, it is not uncommon to find in each marketing plan as many as 50 objectives and many more strategies. This is because of the hierarchy effect of a principal marketing objective leading to a number of sub-objectives, with each of these sub-objectives leading to further sub-objectives. It is rare, however, to find any kind of prioritisation of these objectives, and even rarer to find any allocation of time resource to each. The result is that managers can, and do, get sucked into the day-to-day 'in tray' syndrome, which in turn results in the creeping non-implementation of the marketing plan.

The key role of senior management is to concentrate lower-level management attention on factors that are both high leverage and actionable in order to get the essential jobs done effectively.

To prevent managers getting sidetracked by trivia, the author has found that it is helpful to ask them to prioritise their next year's objectives using a time allocation planner. This is illustrated in Figure 3.11. The principle then is as follows: ensure that all objectives are prioritised according to their impact on the organisation and their urgency, and that resources are allocated accordingly.

	Minor	9	8	6
Impact	Significant	7	5	3
	Major	4	2	1
		Low	Medium	High

Urgency

Key: Possible time/resource allocation (%)		
1 – 30	4 – 12	7 – 8
2 – 15	5 – 10	8 – 4
3 – 12	6 – 8	9 – 1
–	–	–
57	30	13
–	–	–

Figure 3.11 Objectives priority matrix

Hostile corporate cultures

During the years 1985 and 1986, Leppard carried out a research study to attempt to provide an explanation for the widespread corporate resistance to marketing planning.[27] This showed that the acceptance of marketing planning is largely conditioned by the stage of development of the organisation and the behaviour of the corporate culture carriers. Thus it is that different modes of marketing planning became more appropriate at different phases of an organisation's life.

That organisations experience different phases of life as they grow and mature, and that each phase has a different 'life-force', can be explained briefly here (a fuller explanation follows in Chapter 4). Essentially, an organisation is a man-made product, and like all other products will have a finite useful life-cycle. Equally the organisational life-cycle can be extended, if it is managed astutely, just as with products or services. Therefore it is important to recognise when corrective action is required to renew the organisation, and the nature of the appropriate action to take.

All organisations start life because somebody had a 'good idea' and the wherewithal to bring it alive. Sometimes the business idea proves to be the proverbial lead balloon and doesn't get off the ground. However, with good fortune, a following wind and sensible management, the organisation can grow and thrive. Indeed, its very success carries with it the seeds of destruction, because inevitably the organisation outgrows the capabilities of the entrepreneur who gave it birth and was the single 'big brain' running things. One day, an extra customer, an additional order, another machine in the factory, one extra employee, becomes the straw to break the camel's back. The erstwhile busy owner-manager becomes over-loaded and can no longer cope. As a result, the organisation stalls and can go into a tail-spin.

The solution to the problem would be for the owner-manager to take on some specialist staff and to delegate responsibility to them. However, for many entrepreneurs, to let go of even a single string is alien to them. They do not sit comfortably in a formally structured situation – deep down many of them are just not organisational men. They are hunters, rather than farmers, a point that was made earlier.

So here we have an organisation which has enjoyed a relatively trouble-free period of evolutionary growth being confronted with a major crisis. What happens next? There are three possible outcomes:

1. The organisation fails.
2. The owner-manager learns to change his operating style.

3.   A new strong leader appears on the scene.

Either of the last two outcomes enable the organisation to extend its life-cycle, but just as before, the next phase of evolutionary growth also brings with it the germ of the next crisis. In this way, an organisation's total life can be depicted as a series of evolutionary growth phases, interspersed with periodic crisis points:

1.   The first evolutionary growth phase can be termed the organisation's creative evolution. Its momentum is fuelled by the creativity behind the initial business idea, and the creative and flexible manner in which it responds to its business problems.
2.   The first crisis is that of leadership, as we have seen.
3.   The next evolution phase is brought about by a strong figure giving a directive lead. This person clarifies who does what and creates order out of the chaos. He or she will set up rules and procedures and, by doing so, alter the culture which was indigenous to the earlier phase.
4.   The next crisis arrives when the directive leader no longer has the confidence of those working for him or her. As the organisation has grown, so have those in specialist positions grown in expertise. The sales people know more about customers than the chief executive, the technologists are more in touch with the latest developments, and so on. The strong leader who could once give direction and maintain organisational momentum, no longer has credibility, he or she has lost touch. Thus the company is plunged into the autonomy crisis. Whose hand should be on the tiller is the underlying issue.
5.   The crisis is resolved by recognising that the company's expertise must be tapped. Thus more power and authority is delegated to key people throughout the organisation and a period of delegated growth ensues. Again, with the redistribution of power, the organisational culture changes in subtle ways.
6.   As growth continues, those at the top of the organisation are discomforted by feelings that the organisation is getting out of control, the tail is wagging the dog, as it were. There is a crisis about who is really in control.
7.   The resolution of this crisis comes about by establishing better coordination between those at the top and those at the bottom of the organisation. Again the intention is to harness all the strengths.
8.   Unfortunately, attempts to improve coordination lead to a prolifera-tion of systems and procedures which eventually become counter-productive. Decision-making is slowed down and people see

themselves as subordinate to 'the system'. When this happens, the red-tape, bureaucratic 'crisis' phase has arrived.

9. The only solution, to offer a prospect of getting back on an evolutionary growth track, is to get rid of all the unnecessary trappings which have accumulated over the years. To rely more on open and spontaneous communications, for example, instead of memos written in triplicate; to recognise that it is people working together that achieve results, not impersonal systems. In striving to achieve yet another culture change, the organisation moves into its collaborative evolution phase.

10. As we have seen, each period of evolutionary growth eventually comes to an end. It seems (and this is only speculation) that the next crisis might occur because people 'over-collaborate', that is to say, lose the ability to make individual decisions without consultation, or perhaps some form of collective 'group think' loses touch with the environment within which the organisation operates. At present there is insufficient evidence to say with certainty what the next crisis, or its succeeding evolutionary period, will be. However, one thing is certain, human ingenuity will somehow prevail to extend the corporate life-cycle even further.

With this type of overview of how an organisation grows and develops, it is obvious that it is at its weakest during the crisis phases. An alternative strategy which is sometimes employed by organisations when they reach these critical points is to 'put the clock back'. Of course they cannot do this literally, but they can achieve an analogous result by divisionalising, or breaking the organisation down into smaller units. So, for example, an organisation at the red-tape crisis might reason that when it was smaller, it didn't require all these systems and procedures to coordinate and control activities.

Sometimes such a move can be successful, but generally it only delays the inevitable. Continuing this example, managers who have adapted to a bureaucratic culture often carry it with them into the smaller units. Perhaps the company only grows stronger in the long term by learning to overcome the crises as they arise.

The fact that some managers cannot easily let go of cultures that have served them well in periods of evolutionary growth can sometimes explain why it is necessary to import a new chief executive at critical times. Perhaps there is a strong case to be made that you need the right kind of horses for the different (evolutionary growth) courses.

Can managers who have led a company down a particular path suddenly change track? Is it possible for frogs to become princes? Popular books would claim they can, because this is a much more optimistic message with which to sell copies. However, experienced practitioners and consultants would have some reservations.

If the business pressures on a company are great enough, intelligent behaviour will, of course, win the day, as in the cases of British Airways and Woolworth, quoted earlier. In the meantime, however, standardised, textbook-type marketing planning cannot be imposed on all organisations with an equal chance of success, and most definitely not without the active support and participation of the culture leaders. Such participation must involve feeding back to those who have taken part in the process the total results of their efforts.

As a general rule, the marketing planning process should be matched to the organisation life phases in this way:

- creative evolution – marketing plans are generally absent, but a sales plan will be useful;
- directed evolution – a systematic, top-down process will be most compatible with the corporate culture;
- delegation evolution – a bottom-up marketing planning process;
- coordinated evolution – a combination of top-down, bottom-up; and
- collaborative evolution – a more imaginative, less bureaucratic approach, perhaps only planning around key products or markets (remember the 80:20 rule!)

The final principle then, is as follows: marketing planning will not be effective without the active support and participation of the culture leaders. But even with their support, the type of marketing planning has to be appropriate for the phase of the organisational life line. This phase should be measured before attempting to introduce marketing planning.

CONCLUSION

It will be understood from the foregoing that marketing planning never has been the simple step-by-step approach described so enthusiastically in most prescriptive texts and courses. The moment an organisation embarks on the marketing planning path, it can expect to encounter a number of complex organisational, attitudinal, process and cognitive problems that are likely to block progress. By being forewarned about these barriers, there is a good chance of doing excellent marketing planning that will bring all the claimed benefits, including a significant impact on the bottom line through the creation of competitive advantage.

If they are ignored, however, marketing planning will remain the Cinderella of business management.

APPENDIX: THE DIRECTIONAL POLICY MATRIX

The intention of this appendix is to explore why such a potentially rich tool as the directional policy matrix ('DPM') appears to be so rarely used in the real world of marketing and in the preparation of marketing plans. The author has worked with many directors and senior managers on marketing planning, and only in a few instances has the DPM been used correctly and to any useful effect. These notes are the result of working on the construction of an expert system for marketing planning for the DTI EXMAR Club, for which the author is the principal external expert.[28] The DPM is one of the central tools of this expert system.

It is assumed that the reader is familiar with the origin and development of the DPM, and this appendix will deal in detail with a number of issues which seem to cause problems for very experienced and well-qualified marketing practitioners when they attempt to use a tool which, at the cognitive level, appears straightforward, in their own operational environment. It will begin by discussing a number of comparatively straightforward issues, and will move gradually into the much trickier areas which seem to cause most of the problems.

Definition of strategic business unit ('SBU')

Although this is comparatively easy to deal with, it is rarely explained in prescriptive texts dealing with the DPM. The most commonly accepted definition of an SBU is as follows:

1. It will have common segments and competitors for most of the products.
2. It will be a competitor in an external market.
3. It is a discrete, separate and identifiable ('unit').
4. Its manager will have control over most of the areas critical to success.

The process of defining an SBU can be applied all the way down to product or department level.

Definition of what should be plotted on the matrix

This is also a comparatively simple issue to deal with, although again, some confusion arises because the options are rarely spelled out. Let us take a hypothetical two dimensional '*market*' into which a number of products are sold (see Figure 3.12)

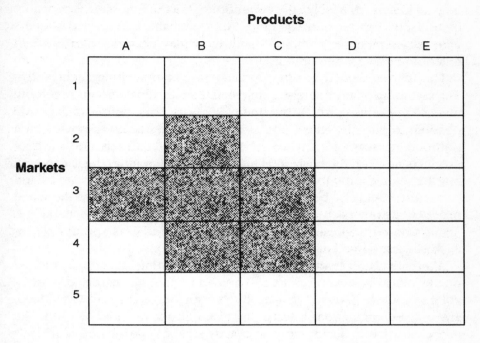

Figure 3.12 The matrix

Each square might be considered as a segment, and various combinations could be considered to be the 'market', as follows:

- the actual product/customer cells served;
- the intersection of product functions ABC and customer groups 2,3,4;
- product functions A,B,C for *all* customer groups;
- customer groups 2,3,4, for *all* product functions;
- the entire matrix.

The lesson here for the use of the DPM is clear. There has to be more than one (we would say at least three, and would suggest a maximum of ten) 'markets' or segments on the vertical axis. These can be either existing markets or potential markets. By definition, therefore, this means that there will be more than one 'product' on the horizontal axis (in the case of the minimum, three). There can be more than three if the planner chooses to plot more than either one product or the aggregation of all products in any served market.

Definitions of 'market' and 'market segment' whilst useful, don't really help all that much to solve the conundrum, but the following is probably quite useful for our purpose here: 'An identifiable group of customers with requirements in common that are, or may become, *significant* in determining a separate strategy'.

The answer, then, is a matter purely of management judgement, and at the beginning of any exercise using the DPM, the most important priority must be to define correctly the unit of analysis. For example, it is clearly possible to put 25 circles (or crosses, where there is no turnover) on a portfolio matrix, with markets 1–5 on the vertical axis and each of products A – E on the horizontal axis (ie the final point in the list above), but that would probably result in a very confusing array of circles and crosses. It would also be possible to put 6 circles on a matrix, (ie the actual product/customer cells served – the first point on the list) with markets 2, 3 and 4 on the vertical axis and products A, B and C as appropriate for each of these served markets on the horizontal axis.

Alternatively, instead of products A, B and C being individually plotted on the critical success factor ('CSF') horizontal axis, an aggregate value or volume could be plotted for all products in any served market. Or, indeed, any of the combinations listed in the example above could be used. The user clearly has to decide early on exactly what will be the unit of analysis for the purpose of determining the size of each circle that will appear in the matrix.

The other lesson concerns an even broader meaning of the word 'market'. It really can mean anything we wish it to mean – eg country, region, division, subsidiary, market, segment, outlet, distributor. The writer has even used it for 'breakfast' attractiveness in the case of a hotel with a problem. The issue of whether products can be plotted on the vertical axis instead of markets will be discussed next.

How to deal with sales into a single market

Recently the writer experienced the interesting case of a senior marketing manager of a blue chip company who dismissed the DMP as irrelevant because he had only four principal products, each one of which was sold to the same customer (or market). Clearly we are talking about major capital sales in this instance.

The manager had plotted products A B C and D on the horizontal axis with only one 'market' on the vertical axis. The resulting matrix obviously had four circles in a straight line. Since the purpose of a matrix is to develop a relationship between two or more variables judged by the planner to be of significance in a given planning context, this matrix was clearly absurd and served no useful purpose whatever. If this manager really wished to use the DPM, he would *have* to put products A, B, C and D on the vertical axis and look at their respective size and strengths on the horizontal axis. In such a case, all we have done is to change the nomenclature, making a product equivalent to a market, which is clearly acceptable. The main point is that the purpose of the DPM is to display clearly and visibly the relationships between product/market variables.

It is certainly possible to use 'product' as 'market', especially in the case such as that first described, for unless the four products are identical in all respects, each would in practice represent a different market to us. This is certainly the case for the Cranfield School of Management portfolio, where product (eg, MBA programme) equals market. Figure 3.13 is a reproduction of the Cranfield portfolio in 1984 showing current (1984) and forecast (1987) positions. (Today, the circles are in different positions – for example, the Executive MBA is much larger and to the left of the matrix as a result of executive action – surely the purpose of using the DPM in the first place!)

How to deal with business strengths/critical success factors (the horizontal axis)

We can now turn to issues which are somewhat more complex and often cause confusion. The first of these concerns the quantification of business strengths in a 'market'.

It is the writer's view that the lists of factors in most books offered for the manager to choose from are not particularly useful when used by *marketing* managers for the purpose of constructing a marketing plan. Few of these factors take account of the need for a company to make an 'offer' to a particular 'market' that has a sustainable competitive advantage over the 'offers' of relevant competitors. The only way a company can do this is to understand the *real* needs and wants of the chosen customer group, find out by means of market research exactly how well these needs are currently being met by the main relevant products on offer, and then seek to satisfy these needs better than their competitors. Figure 3.14 sets out a typical calculation made by a company using a methodology developed by the author to estimate its strength in a market.[29]

From this it will be seen that this organisation is not market leader and all competitors score more than 5.0.

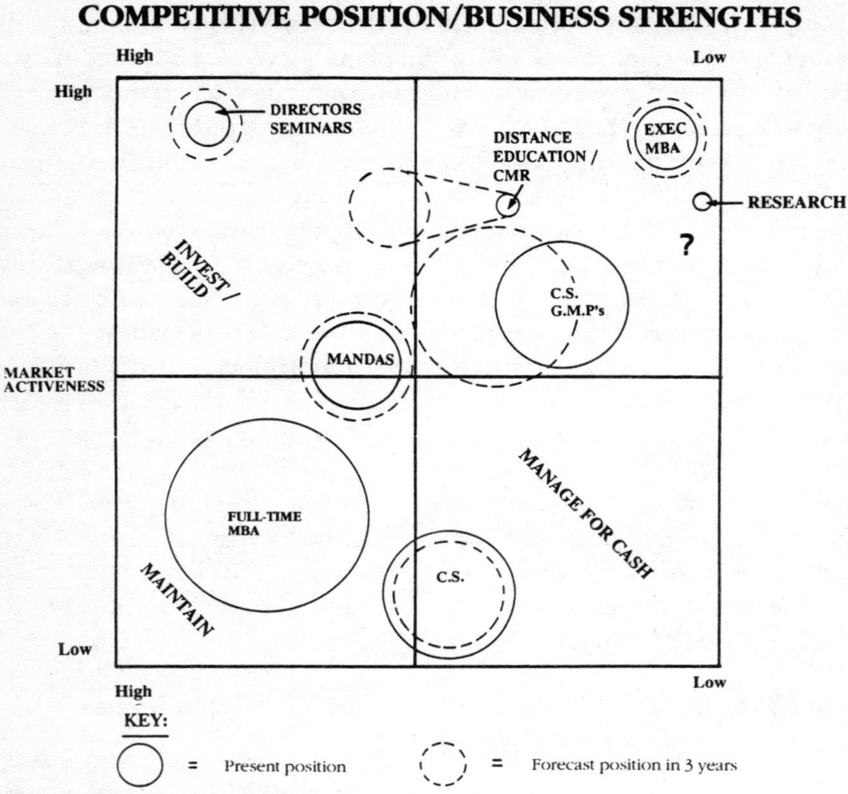

COMPETITIVE POSITION/BUSINESS STRENGTHS

Figure 3.13 School of management product portfolio – competitive position/business strengths

The problem with this and many similar calculations is that rarely will this method discriminate sufficiently well to indicate the relative strengths of a number of products in a particular company's product/market portfolio. Some method, then, is required to prevent all products appearing on the left of the matrix. This can be achieved by using a ratio, as in the Boston matrix. In this case, a ratio will indicate a company's position *relative* to the best in the market.

In the example provided, Competitor A has most strengths in the market, so our organisation probably needs to make some improvements when compared with the 'leader'. To reflect this, our weighted score should be expressed as a ration of Competitor A (the highest weighted score). Thus $6.7 \div 7.8 = 0.86 : 1$. If we were to plot this on a logarithmic scale on the horizontal axis, this would place our organisation to the right of the dividing line. (We should make the left hand extreme point $3 \times$ and

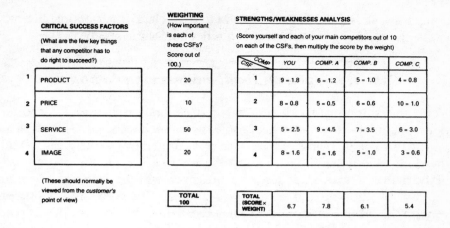

Figure 3.14 Estimating market strength

start the scale on the right at 0.3.) A scale of 3 × to 0.3 has been chosen because such a band is likely to encapsulate most extremes of competitive advantage. If it doesn't, just change it to suit your own industry circumstance.

How to deal with market attractiveness factors

The first time managers try using the DPM they frequently find that the circles do not come out where expected. One possible reason for this is a misunderstanding concerning the use of market attractiveness factors. Please remember, you will be most concerned about the *potential* for *growth in volume, growth in profit*, and so on for your organisation in each of your 'markets'.

For example, even if a 'market' is mature (or even in decline), if the potential is there for your company to grow in this mature market, then it would obviously be more attractive than one in which there was little or no potential for you to grow. (As would be the case, for example if you already had a high market share). Likewise, even if a 'market' is currently very profitable for your company, if there was little or no potential for growing the profit, this 'market' might be considered less attractive than one which was currently not so profitable to your company, but which offered good potential for growing your profits.

Let us have a look at two companies whose revenue and profits were static for two consecutive years, and both of which kept their shareholders at bay by selling off some of their assets. The boards of both companies attempted to use the DPM to help clarify the options. In both cases, the resulting matrix was not a reflection of the reality.

Case 1: An international engineering company

Here, the shipping, food, thermal and separation divisions were all operating in no-growth markets. Only the biotechnology division was in a growth market. Using *market growth* as a factor obviously caused all divisions except the biotechnology division to appear in the bottom half of the matrix. The other factor used, however, was *profitability*, which in the case of shipping and separation was high. The weighting of 60 per cent on the profit factor pulled both of these divisions into the upper part of the matrix. Strengths in each case were different, and the resulting matrix looked as shown in Figure 3.15.

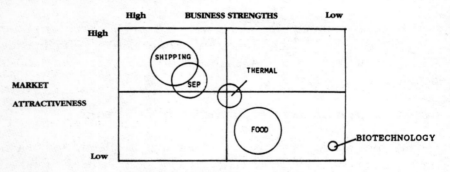

Figure 3.15 The matrix 1

However, since both shipping and separation divisions had little (if any) potential to *grow* their volume and profitability in mature markets, and since food and biotechnology divisions did, the circles were clearly in the wrong place. The *reality* facing the company was as illustrated in Figure 3.16.

The opportunity was clearly there for this company to invest in the food division, where it was comparatively weak, and also in the thermal division. Both of these markets provided ample opportunity for the company to grow its market share and strengths (especially if it also used productivity measures at the same time), in spite of the fact that both markets were relatively mature. In other words, all we are really interested in is the *potential* for us to grow our volume and profits, and in some instances, externally derived factors of market growth and profitability, however accurate, are not particularly useful.

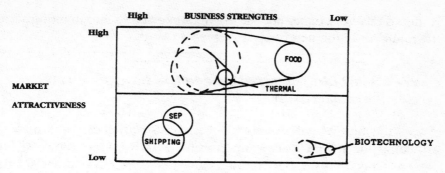

Figure 3.16 The matrix 2

Having reached the conclusion above, obviously this company then took each division in turn and completed the DPM for each of their component parts in order to decide how best to allocate resources.

Case 2: A conglomerate with 12 separate companies

This group, although enjoying very high ROCE, was also under extreme pressure from the financial institutions because its turnover and profits were static. At a directors' meeting, the DPM was used as one of the basic tools of analysis. ROCE of the companies varied between 500 per cent and 5 per cent, with 7 above 50 per cent and 5 below 15 per cent.

Again, using market growth and industry ROS as the factors, weighted 30 and 70, not surprisingly, all the high profit companies appeared in the top left of the matrix and all the low profit companies appeared in the bottom half of the matrix. All this did was to confirm the group's existing position, but was of little value when considering the future.

The author advised the directors to change the factors to encapsulate *potential* for growth in volume and profits rather than the inherent growth and profitability of the markets themselves. The resulting DPM then showed most of the high profit companies in the lower half of the matrix, since few of them were in growth markets and most already had high market shares. It also demonstrated clearly another point of policy. One company enjoying a 500 per cent ROCE could grow, providing the chairman was prepared to allow them to redefine their market more broadly and move into lower ROS segments. Such a policy move would have put this particular company back into the top part of the matrix!

But this, of course, is the whole point of using the DPM in the first place.

It should raise key issues and force senior executives into thinking about the future in a structured way.

Circle positioning at some time in the future: can the circles move vertically?

'No' is the best answer, although 'yes' is also an acceptable answer, providing the matrix shows the current level of attractiveness at the present time. This implies carrying out one set of calculations for the present time according to the agreed market attractiveness factors, in order to locate markets on the vertical axis, then carrying out another set of calculations for a future period (say, in three years' time), based on forecasts according to the same market attractiveness factors.

In practice, it is quicker and easier to carry out only the latter calculation, in which case the circles can only move horizontally. This makes *No* the more likely answer.

Circle positioning at some time in the future: can market attractiveness factors change while constructing a DPM?

'No', of course, is the correct answer. Once agreed, under no circumstances should market attractiveness factors be changed, otherwise the attractiveness of our markets is not being evaluated against common criteria and the matrix becomes meaningless. Scores, however, will be specific to each market.

Please note, however, that you must list the 'markets' that you intend to apply the criteria to before deciding on the criteria themselves, since the purpose of the vertical axis is to discriminate between more and less attractive 'markets'. This will prevent all your 'markets' appearing in the top half of the matrix, which would clearly make the exercise pointless. The criteria themselves, therefore, must be specific to the population of 'markets' under consideration and, once agreed, must not be changed for different 'markets' in the same population.

The author was recently working with a group of senior managers in an international steel company. They defined market attractiveness factors correctly, weighted each one accordingly, and then proceeded to put through only their five top markets. Not surprisingly, all appeared in the top left of the matrix! If they intended to use only their top performing markets, then clearly they should have devised criteria that would have discriminated only between those five markets.

Conclusion

It will be readily grasped from the foregoing discussion why the DPM can so easily be misused and misunderstood, in spite of the technique being described in most basic marketing texts and being taught on many basic marketing programmes. The fault appears to lie more with those responsible for writing about and teaching the subject than with those who try to use it. Similar problems caused the somewhat simpler Boston Consulting Group matrix to fall into misuse.

The author has written two computer-based training programs, one on the BCG and one on the DPM. Both feature a case study and ask the 'student' to work through the methodology, using the data provided. A self-scoring system is provided in each program. Having put over 1000 students and practising managers through these programs, the author is convinced that both methodologies are just as valuable today as when their creators first introduced them into an excited business world. The ultimate proof came one day when a competent postgraduate teacher, having been through both computer programs, approached the author and said: 'Do you know, I have been teaching the BCG matrix and the DPM for seven years, and this is the first time I've really understood them and realised their true potential.' In particular, the DPM is especially powerful. It should not be allowed to die because of ignorance.

REFERENCES

1. McDonald, M H B (1984) *Theory and Practice of Marketing Planning for Industrial Goods in International Markets*, Cranfield Institute of Technology, PhD.
2. Thompson, S (1962) *How Companies Plan*, AMA Research Study, No 54, AMA.
3. Kollatt, D J, Blackwell, R D and Robeson, J F (1972) *Strategic Marketing*, Holt, Rinehart and Winston, New York.
4. Ansoff, H I (1977) 'The state and practice of planning systems', *Sloan Management Review*, 18(2), Winter.
5. Thune, S and House, R (1970) 'Where long-range planning pays off', *Business Horizons*, 7(4), August.
6. Leighton, D S R (1966) *International Marketing Text and Cases*, McGraw-Hill, New York.
7. Wong, V, Saunders, J and Doyle P (1988) 'The quality of British marketing: a comparative investigation of international competition in the UK market',

Proceedings of the 21st Annual Conference of Marketing Education Group, Huddersfield Polytechnic, July, Butterworth-Heinemann, Oxford.

8. King, S (1983) *Applying Research to Decision Making*, presented at the MRS Conference, Spring.

9. Evered, R (1981) 'Management education in the year 2000', in Cooper, C L (ed) *Developing Managers for the 1980s*, Macmillan, London.

10. Hughes, J (1988) 'The body and knowledge in management education', *Management Education and Development*, 19, 301–310.

11. Schon, D (1984) *The Crisis of Professional Knowledge and the Pursuit of an Epistemology of Practice*, research paper for Harvard Business School.

12. McBurnie, A (1988) 'The need for a new marketing perspective', *MBA Review*, 1(1), March.

13. Rangaswamy, A, Burke, R A, Wind, J and Eliashberg, J (1988) *Expert Systems for Marketing*, Marketing Science Institution Working Paper Report Nos 87–107.

14. Reid, D M and Hinkley, L C (1989) 'Strategic planning: the cultural impact', *Marketing Intelligence and Planning*, 7, 11.

15. Leppard, J and McDonald, M H B (1987) 'A reappraisal of the role of marketing planning', *Journal of Marketing Management*, 3(2).

16. Kotler, P (1988) *Marketing Management: Analysis, Planning, Implementation and Control*, 6th edn, Prentice-Hall, Englewood Cliffs NJ.

17. Doyle, P (1989) 'Building successful brands: the strategic options', *Journal of Marketing Management*, 5(1).

18. McDonald, M H B (1990) 'Some methodological problems associated with the directional policy matrix', *MBA Review*, Spring.

19. Speed, R J (1989) 'Oh Mr Porter: a reappraisal of competitive strategy', *Marketing Intelligence and Planning*, 6(5).

20. Reid, D M and Hinkley, L C (1989) op cit.

21. Peters, T J and Waterman, R H (1982) *In Search of Excellence*, Harper and Row, New York.

22. McDonald, M H B (1989a) 'Marketing planning and expert systems: an epistemology of practice', *Marketing Intelligence and Planning*, 7(7/8).

23. Lock, A R and Hughes, D R (1989) 'Soft information systems for marketing decision support', *Marketing Intelligence and Planning*, 17(11).

24. Strategic Planning Institute (1986) *Membership Conference Keynote Address*, Cambridge, Mass.

25. Gorb, P (1978) 'Management development for the small firm', *Personnel Management*, January.

26. Leppard, J W (1987) *Marketing Planning and Corporate Culture*, Cranfield Institute of Technology, M. Phil.

27. Leppard, J W (1987) op cit.

28. McDonald, M H B (1989a) op cit.

29. McDonald, M H B (1989b) *Marketing Plans: How to Prepare Them, How to Use Them*, Butterworth-Heinemann, Oxford.

4

An Investigation of Management Attitudes in the Context of Marketing Planning*

OVERVIEW

The purpose of this chapter is to explore further some of the organisational and people issues introduced in Chapter 2. It examines the marketing planning process of a number of British companies and finds that the companies who subscribe to what is described here as a 'complete marketing planning process' are further along an organisational evolutionary development path than their semi-planning and non-planning counterparts.

While the marketing planning process appears on the surface to be just a series of procedural steps, it does in fact embrace a set of underlying values and assumptions. Only the more developed and mature organisations seem likely to have the corporate culture which is capable of sustaining these values. Corporate culture is often intangible to the outsider, but can be very real to those within the company. It develops partly through the way the company has triumphed over adversity in the past, and partly through the so-called 'culture carriers'. These are the influential figures who, by their behaviour, communicate the organisatio-

---

* This chapter is reproduced with the permission of the Academic Press Inc, London. It first appeared in the *Journal of Marketing Management*, volume 7, number 3, July 1991 as 'Marketing Planning and Corporate Culture: A Conceptual framework which Examines Management Attributes in the Context of Marketing Planning'.

nal values they wish to see espoused. Because marketing planning often challenges existing corporate values and attempts to introduce new ones, the process cannot be regarded simply as a neutral, cognitive activity; it is clearly a political process. The problems this poses for executives of organisations and their external advisers are complex and far-reaching. Nevertheless, the potential rewards which result from comprehensive marketing planning can be substantial, and make it a goal worth striving for.

INTRODUCTION

It is generally accepted that marketing planning is 'a good thing'. Indeed, a number of benefits are promised for those who invest in this process. As early as 1962, Thompson[1] provided sufficient evidence to conclude that marketing planners 'will always outperform those who do not plan'. In 1974 Schoeffler et al[2] added that marketing planning is 'A systematic approach to strategy formulation which leads to a higher return on investment.' Other benefits were discussed in detail in Chapter 2.

Yet, surprisingly, more recent studies that have been carried out in the UK, one by McDonald (1984)[3] and one by Greenley (1985)[4] that reviewed four UK studies of marketing planning, provide evidence that as few as 10 per cent of companies actually use what might be called a comprehensive marketing process. Even the most optimistic of these studies could offer only a figure of 25 per cent.

Thus, the situation is something of a paradox. On the one hand, there is a body of evidence to suggest that there are some very real and worthwhile benefits to be gained from marketing planning. On the other hand, very few British companies appear to invest in this process. It was the wish to understand more about the reasons why marketing planning is rejected by a majority of companies that provided the stimulus for the thesis on which this chapter is based (Leppard, 1987).[5]

INITIAL CONSIDERATIONS, RESEARCH OBJECTIVES, DESIGN AND TERMINOLOGY

Possible reasons for the low acceptance of marketing planning

At the outset of the research programme, there seemed to be several possible explanations for the low level of acceptance of marketing planning.

Marketing planning is too theoretical

Wills (1976)[6] puts forward the idea that business schools should operate at a more theoretical level than industry and commerce as a whole. By doing so, they will find new solutions to business problems that would elude the busy manager who is focused on day-to-day activities. Perhaps then, the abstractions of academia have created an unbridgeable gap for the practitioners in industry?

The marketing planning process is, however, relatively easy to understand at a cognitive level. At its simplest level, it involves a situation review, the setting of objectives and the strategies for achieving them, and ultimately the scheduling and costing out of the necessary actions in the short term to achieve these goals. Moreover, a number of companies manage to use it and so the claim that it might be too theoretical does not appear to hold water.

Senior executives are suspicious of conceptual ideas

There might be some validity in this claim, although Katz (1974)[7] maintains that it is essential for conceptualisation to be a large component of the senior executive's job. If the executive is not capable of functioning in this area, perhaps it is a reflection of the way he/she perceives the executive's role, or of poor selection. Yet again, however, it is difficult to accept this as an explanation in view of the relative simplicity of marketing planning as a process.

There are barriers to learning

Boydell (1977)[8] has identified a number of barriers to learning which could perhaps inhibit the acceptance of marketing planning. These can be termed:

- Perceptual – not seeing that there is a problem.
- Cultural – being trapped within an existing set of ideas with respect to what is right or wrong, good or bad, etc.
- Intellectual – not having the 'ammunition' to cope.
- Emotional – related to personal insecurity and typified by a reluctance to change or take risks.
- Expressive – poor communication skills which limit the ability to explain problems and difficulties to others.
- Environmental – whether or not the 'climate' is supportive or hostile to the conditions necessary for improved performance.

This suggests that there might be barriers to marketing planning that are more than a cognitive or intellectual process. Cultural and environmental factors could equally block marketing planning or reduce its effectiveness.

It is not treated seriously enough

If learning is seen as a problem-solving process, then, as van Boeschoten (1975)[9] suggests, it can be perceived at three levels. Applying his ideas to marketing planning, it is possible to describe the process as follows:

- Level 1 – an unthinking mechanical process, merely a prescription to be followed.
- Level 2 – a complex process which could require the company to develop new procedures and systems, even to invest in new resources to sustain these new developments.
- Level 3 – a process which asks fundamental questions of the company and as a result could affect the nature of the business and its future direction.

Initial hypotheses and research objectives

As a development from these initial ideas, the following hypotheses were put forward:

1. A complete marketing planning process is not simply a series of action steps. It also embodies a set of values and assumptions which, while not being explicit, are nevertheless an integral part of the whole process.
2. Similarly, an organisation is not just a conglomeration of people and resources. It, too, embodies particular values and assumptions which give rise to its distinctive corporate climate and culture. Moreover, its culture would appear to be influenced to some degree by its level of learning or maturity.
3. If the underlying values of a complete marketing planning process are more or less consistent with those of the organisation, then there is a high probability that the planning process would be adopted.
4. If there is a conflict of values between those underlying the marketing planning process and those of the organisation, then it could be expected that the planning process would be rejected.
5. An organisation will not change its values system or culture unless something very significant takes place to make such a change seem worthwhile.

The overall research objective was to test out these initial hypotheses, which might be best summarised as '. . . to improve the understanding about the relationship between an organisation's culture and the marketing planning processes it uses.' It was felt that any new light that could be shed on this area would be particularly useful to both educators and marketing practitioners alike.

Research design

Since the thesis on which this chapter is based was concerned with intangible topics such as corporate culture and management attitudes, it was decided to make the design largely exploratory and phenomenological. Such an illuminative approach, advocated by Glaser and Strauss (1967),[10] made it possible to adapt to unexpected contingencies as the research progressed.

The main source of data was through the use of comprehensive case studies prepared by MBA students at Cranfield and by the researchers themselves. The criteria for selecting these were that they were sufficiently explicit about the company's marketing planning process, cultural background and the problems the company was experiencing. Additional data were collected from in-company management workshops run by the researchers and from questionnaires completed by company personnel.

Because of the in-depth information required, it was necessary to limit the database of companies and to concentrate on quality rather than quantity of information. Nevertheless the case cluster case study analysis method proposed by McClintock (1979)[11] proved to be a useful tool, but the relatively small sample size of 34 companies made too much emphasis on statistical data somewhat irrelevant.

In an attempt to overcome distortion which could be introduced by using one particular analytical technique or questionnaire, whenever possible a 'battery' of approaches was used. Such multi-operationalism reduced the prospect of inherent biases of any one method 'polluting' the end results. Indeed, any bias introduced by one approach would be cancelled out by the inherent biases of the others.

Terminology

Although the marketing planning process can be represented diagrammatically, as in Figure 4.1, it is not necessarily the straightforward, linear sequential operation that the diagram suggests. In reality, all the stages are highly interactive and the planning process requires the flexibility to move backwards and forwards from the general to the specific. Sometimes it is even possible for some stages in the planning process to be dealt with concurrently.

Marketing plans can also vary in their time scale and degree of complexity, both of which will be dependent upon the nature of the host company and its business. Another variable is the degree of formality of the plan. Should it be formalised as Camillus (1975)[12] advocates, thereby making executives 'communicate, think ahead and so on', or should companies heed the warning of Ames (1968)[13] who found that 'an overemphasis on format and procedure leads to a lack of substance and innovative thinking'?

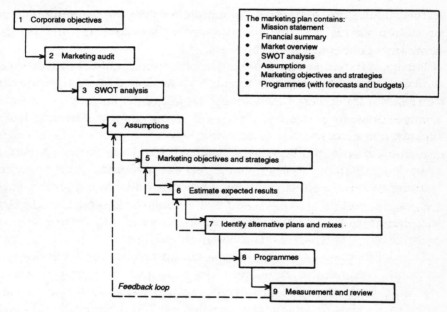

Figure 4.1 The marketing planning process

Clearly marketing planning has to be tailored to suit the style and situation of the company, while steering a course between the Scylla of good intentions and the Charybdis of bureaucracy.

Nevertheless it is possible to describe a marketing planning process which is more or less universally accepted:

1. There is an information gathering stage which addresses itself to the company's internal operations and its external environment (the marketing audit).

2. The major strengths, weaknesses, opportunities and threats are identified from the marketing audit (the SWOT analysis).
3. Basic assumptions are made about the company and its situation.
4. Marketing objectives are set for the business, taking into account the foregoing three steps.
5. Strategies are devised about how best to attain the marketing objectives.
6. Programmes are formulated which identify timing, responsibilities and costs.
7. The marketing plan is monitored and reviewed at regular intervals.

In this chapter, any reference to a complete marketing planning process or system means that the above seven stages have featured in the company's deliberations.

Finally, agreeing a suitable definition of corporate culture proved quite difficult. Depending on which researcher's work one studies, culture can be 'observable behaviour regularities', 'language', 'a philosophy', 'rules of a game for getting accepted', 'physical layout' or 'ways by which the organisation relates with outsiders', and so on.

Eventually, a definition given by Schein (1983)[14] was chosen: 'A pattern of basic assumptions that a given group has invented or developed in learning to cope with its problems of external adaptation and internal integration, and that have worked well enough to be considered valid, and therefore, to be taught to new members as the correct way to perceive, think and feel in relation to these problems.'

This definition underlies the complexity and breadth of the concept of corporate culture. Also, by implication, it suggests that cultures are, by and large, backward-looking and conservative, in the sense that they are based on successful coping strategies that worked in the past.

Already an interesting scenario was developing from these two crucial definitions. Marketing planning was a forward-looking process, whereas corporate culture seemed to have its origins in the past. Would it be possible to accommodate these two different time orientations into this research frame of reference?

DESK RESEARCH AND LITERATURE REVIEW

This part of the research set out to explore two main areas:

1. To examine the marketing planning process and to establish what underlying assumptions could be made about a company using this process.

2. To identify some of the key determinants of corporate culture from the world of management and organisational development.

The overall objective was to develop conceptual frameworks about marketing planning and corporate values which could be tested in the field.

Analysis of the marketing planning process

An adapted version of the skills analysis technique developed by Seymour (1968)[15] was applied to each step of the planning process. This meant that each step was considered in terms of its implications regarding knowledge, skill and underlying assumptions. An example of the way in which this technique was applied to the first two stages of the planning process is given in Table 4.1.

Table 4.1 Example of an analysis of the marketing planning process

Process step	Knowledge	Skill	Underlying assumptions
1. Set corporate objectives	Knowledge about: a) corporate planning b) setting objectives	Ability to: a) produce a corporate plan b) set corporate objectives	a) The organisation possesses the required knowledge and skills b) It sees a need for a corporate plan c) The corporate plan is used to 'direct' sub-objectives d) The corporate plan specifies corporate objectives in five areas: marketing, production, finance, distribution, personnel e) The corporate plan is authoritative enough to be believed f) There are adequate resources allocated to planning

Process step	Knowledge	Skill	Underlying assumptions
2. Conduct marketing audit	Knowledge about: a) marketing systems b) audit theory c) source of information d) product life cycle analysis e) various analytical 'tools', eg customer, segmentation, benefit analysis, gap analysis, Boston Consulting Group matrix, etc	The ability to: a) critically appraise all steps of the marketing system b) separate fact from opinion c) use analytical tools in a workmanlike manner	a) That required knowledge and skill exist b) There is a willingness to appraise the marketing operation c) Data exist which make this possible d) Somebody (or group) has the responsibility to conduct the audit e) Time is made available for the audit to be conducted f) It is a critical process which genuinely strives for improvement rather than for maintaining the status quo

The total analysis of the planning process enabled the following conclusions to be drawn. A company will only be able to produce a complete marketing plan if:

1. It has the required body of knowledge, the bulk of which is concerned with understanding planning, marketing and various conceptual, analytical marketing tools.
2. It can translate this knowledge into practical working skills and procedures.
3. Adequate resources are allocated to the planning process in terms of people, time and back-up support.
4. There is an adequate data bank and data retrieval system.
5. The plan or planning process is perceived as necessary and not wasteful of time and effort – ie there is a belief in planning.
6. There is a corporate plan to provide a context for the marketing plan.
7. Personnel are willing to own up to problems or disclose where existing situations could be improved.
8. Roles are made clear regarding who does what.

9. Facts outweigh opinions.
10. Senior executives value and pay due cognisance to the information that emerges from the planning process, to the extent that they will act upon it.

Overall it would seem that such a company sees marketing to be an important function and addresses the implications of being marketing orientated in a mature and rational manner.

Another way of looking at these conclusions is to assume that if any of the factors listed were to be absent, or inadequate in some way, then the whole marketing planning process would suffer. In this sense, all of the items listed above can be potential barriers to success. Moreover, this list can be further distilled as shown below.

Barriers to marketing planning

The barriers to marketing planning were identified as:

- Cognitive – inadequate knowledge and skills (from conclusion 1 above).
- Information – lack of appropriate data (from conclusions 2, 4 and 9 above).
- Resource – inadequate allocation of people, time, money, etc (from conclusion 3 above).
- Cultural – lack of belief in planning and/or marketing (from conclusions 5, 7, and 10 above).
- Behavioural – people will act inappropriately, eg, fail to disclose valuable information or act upon it (from conclusions 2 and 8 above).

Intellectually it seemed reasonable to surmise that of these five domains, or potential barriers to marketing planning, cognition would be central. Without the anchor of cognition, all the other domains would have nothing to hold them in place.

Such consideration of these barriers to marketing planning led to the initial conceptual model of an organisation as shown in Figure 4.2. What this is intended to convey is that each domain has an interdependence with all the others. The effectiveness of the marketing planning process will depend on the extent to which all the component parts of the model are developed to play their part. Undue emphasis or neglect in one component would lead to imbalance in the total effort. In essence, this model is a snapshot of the organisation as it is poised between its historical past and its future goals. It was hoped that the literature review would validate and build on this initial model.

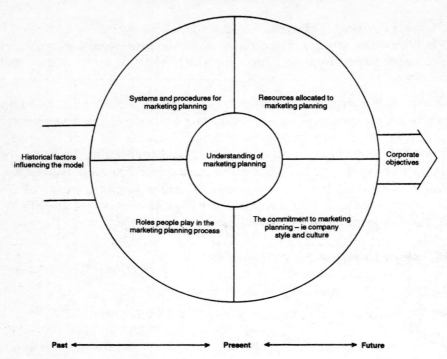

Figure 4.2 Conceptual model of organisation: initial configuration

Literature review

McDonald (1984)[16] identified several factors which he believed had a strong influence on a company's ability to introduce and develop a complete marketing planning process. These were: management style; company size; its structure; and its culture. Each of these factors was considered in some detail.

Management style

There appear to be many different ways to look at management style, but in the end, attention focused on only the better-researched theories. These were:

- the Blake-Mouton grid (1964)[17] – ie concern for output versus concern for people;
- Lickert (1967)[18] – ie autocratic–democratic continuum;
- Hersey and Blanchard (1977)[19] – ie situational leadership; and
- McClelland (1970)[20] – ie sociability, power and achievement motivation.

Since all of these approaches addressed the issue of management style or behaviour, it was possible to identify some correlation between them. How they appear to relate is shown in Figure 4.3.

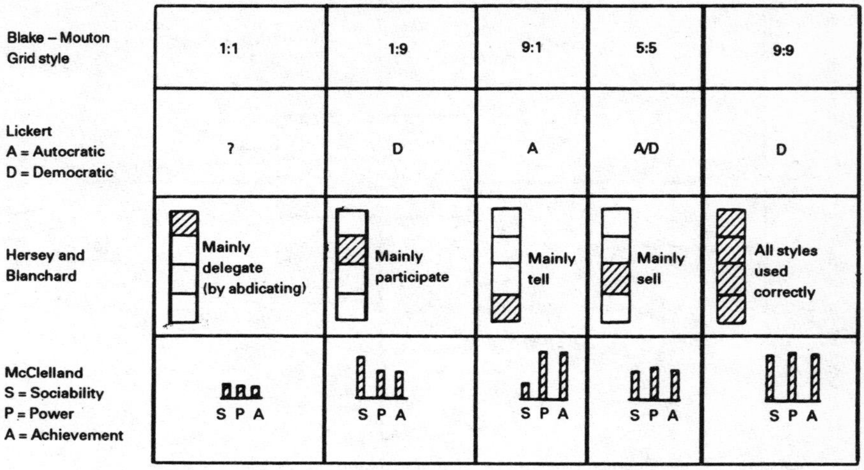

	1:1	1:9	9:1	5:5	9:9
Blake – Mouton Grid style					
Lickert A = Autocratic D = Democratic	?	D	A	A/D	D
Hersey and Blanchard	Mainly delegate (by abdicating)	Mainly participate	Mainly tell	Mainly sell	All styles used correctly
McClelland S = Sociability P = Power A = Achievement	S P A	S P A	S P A	S P A	S P A

Figure 4.3 Synthesis of the various ideas about management style

The significance of this synthesis of theories on management style is two-fold. Not only is the style approximating to 9:9 on the Blake-Mouton grid, the most effective, but it is also the style most descriptive of behaviour in the 'mature company', or in other words, the style most likely to sustain a complete marketing planning system. This disclosure led to a speculative model of marketing planning styles using the grid format as shown in Figure 4.4.

Company size

Many writers have observed that as a company grows and learns to cope with new problems associated with its increased size and success, it also changes in character. Lievegoed (1973)[21] identifies three quite distinct phases of organisational life which he terms pioneer, differentiated (or scientific) and integrated. Greiner (1972)[22] has similar views, but suggests that there are a number of evolutionary growth periods in a company's life, each followed by a revolutionary crisis phase which signifies that the period of natural growth is over. These are illustrated in Figure 4.5.

Normann (1977)[23] and Bhattachary (1981)[24] view company size in a different way and see growth as being a reflection of the stage of development along a life-cycle curve. For Normann, the subject for the

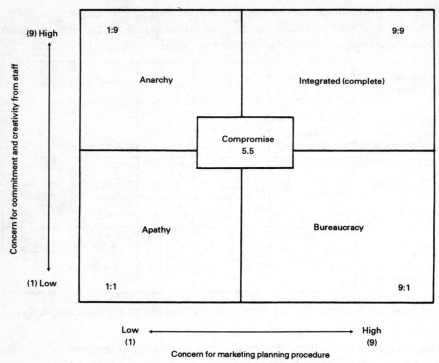

Figure 4.4 Styles of marketing planning

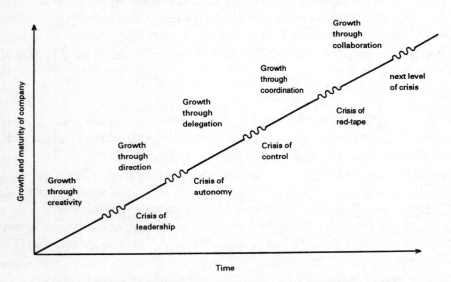

Figure 4.5 Greiner's stages of evolution and revolution

life-cycle is the business idea itself and clearly this is capable of being modified and adapted in the light of experience. Bhattachary, on the other hand, claims that the company overall has a life-cycle and has the capability of passing through a period of early struggle, to one of motivation, followed by complacency and ultimately decline. In his terms, organizational renewal is not an easy option.

Structure

In essence, the structuralists seek to find rational ways to build an organisational structure best suited to match the company to its chosen environment. Burns and Stalker (1961)[25] found that in stable environments the so-called mechanistic organisation (bureaucratic, impersonal, formal communication channels and a high division of labour), was more successful than what they termed the 'organic' organisation (non-bureaucratic, informal with multi-path communication channels). When the environment became more volatile, however, the reverse was true.

Lawrence and Lorsch (1967)[26] took a different view and put forward their ideas about differentiated and integrated companies, differentiation being the degree of separateness within the total organisation of the various systems, subsystems and specialist functions. Integration was the process of achieving unity of effort among these various subsystems, in the accomplishment of the organisation's goals. They claimed that the amount of differentiation and integration should relate to that of the company's environment.

The structuralists, however, do not appear to accept the possibility that the way an organisation is shaped is often the result of political ambitions of senior executives who have sufficient power and influence.

Culture and politics

A number of works were studied and the following overall conclusions were drawn:

1. A company's history has a significant impact on its culture and, because of this, influences many of the decisions which are made.
2. A company's learning is inextricably tied up with its history, as a result of things that have worked, or problems that have been overcome, in the past.
3. Senior executives are the 'culture carriers' and as such can either reinforce or work to change the existing culture.
4. Organisational myths and heroes sustain the culture and with it the existing political power structure.

5. A shared values system can be a source of strength and commitment to the company.
6. The more explicit are the values system and organisational vision, the more committed are the staff.
7. Culture only has to be 'sensible' to those who operate within the company. It doesn't necessarily have to be rational or congruent with the current business environment.
8. The more deeply a culture is embedded, the more difficult it is to change.

Thus, corporate cultures can be anti-developmental, since they are backward-looking. Equally, it takes a senior executive with vision and high commitment to overthrow an out-of-date culture and replace it with a new set of more appropriate norms of behaviour.

This idea of trying to change the corporate culture opened up a new avenue of exploration.

Perspectives on organisational change

Mangham (1979)[27] and Marshall and McLean (1985)[28] found that corporate culture created an inertia which reduced attempts to introduce radical change into something far less potent, and consequently, less effective. Johnson (1984)[29] found that a successful change process had to start with the existing cultural norms being loosened and their culture carriers discredited. This paves the way for a subsequent reconstruction, which ultimately allows for consolidation into a new cultural recipe. Williams (1970)[30] discovered that for the change process to be managed to a successful conclusion, several different rules needed to be played. These are termed:

- Change agent – the person who stimulates the change, either from inside the organisation, or as an external adviser.
- Catalyst – a person with enough power to ensure the change takes place, but who might well remain unaffected at a personal level.
- Pacemaker – the person who provides the energy to keep the change process going.
- Diffusion agent(s) – who help to transfer or communicate the change into the furthest recesses of the organisation.

The influence of the various role players assumes different importance as the change process unfolds, as shown in Figure 4.6.

Schein (1985)[31] claims that there are a number of different ways of intervening in a company in order to bring about a change in corporate culture. By and large, these intervention techniques need to be matched

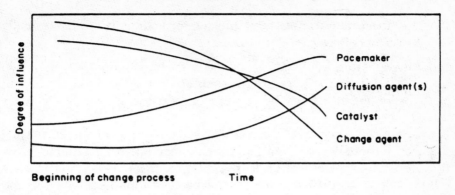

Figure 4.6 Influences of role players during the change process (after Williams)

to the company's stage of development and are required to be increasingly coercive, the stronger the existing culture is embedded.

His study of culture carriers identified five main observable actions that leaders take, either consciously or subconsciously, which transmit and embed culture. These primary mechanisms are:

1. How the leader reacts to crises or critical incidents.
2. The criteria they establish for allocating rewards and status.
3. The areas to which the leader pays attention, measures and controls.
4. The criteria they establish for recruitment, selection, promotion, retirement and dismissing staff.
5. The role model the leader promotes by either their own behaviour, or by coaching and teaching others.

Schein also identified a second tier of cultural transmitters, which are:

1. Organisational systems and procedures.
2. Organisational design and structure.
3. Design of physical space, façades and buildings.
4. Formal statements about organisational philosophy, creeds and charters.
5. Stories, legends, myths and parables about important people and events in the company's life.

Key issues from the literature review

Overall, it seems that there are two main determinants of corporate culture:

1. The culture that has evolved as the company developed and which is related to its maturity or stage of development.

2. The 'culture' promoted by the senior executive or an equally powerful culture carrier or group.

From the literature review it appears that the most potent of these two forces is the former. The reasons for this are not difficult to see and can perhaps be illustrated best by comparing this process to an individual's development.

Imagine the exasperated parents of a rebellious teenage son. They might try exhortation or a number of other strategies to get him to 'grow up' and 'act like an adult'. But clearly, growing up and becoming an adult can only be achieved in the fullness of time. Any adult-like behaviour the parents manage to induce in their offspring at this earlier stage is likely to be a veneer of little substance. They tend to forget that before this current stage of development, their son was in turn an adventurous toddler and a compliant child. These stages were not inherently better or worse than any other, just different.

Equally true, however, is the fact that the son cannot permanently live in some kind of time-warp and remain an eternal teenager, pleasant though the prospects of doing so might appear to him. Time passing and accrued experience are two factors that nobody (and that includes organisations), can sidestep and avoid.

Like the wise parent, the chief executive will recognise when his charge is ready to grow into another phase of development and will act accordingly. He will not try to keep the growing organisation in the equivalent of short trousers, but nor will he rush into trying to make it into something that is impossible to attain at the time. As the literature has shown, organisations have their own built-in mechanisms for dealing with change. Often the culture carrier is not an agent for development, but merely an upholder of past tradition.

There are, of course, dangers in carrying analogies too far. Unlike individuals, organisations have the potential to renew themselves and in theory they could last forever. However, as none seem to be immortal, it was felt that this idea of stages of organisational development was well worth examining in more detail, especially in terms of how it correlated with the marketing planning processes of the company.

RESEARCH FINDINGS AND CONCLUSIONS

Designing a measuring instrument

After much experimentation, an instrument in the form of a questionnaire was designed. Since it was required to illuminate the organisational context within which marketing planning operated, this instrument needed to have a reasonably 'well-graduated scale'. That is to say, one which could, with some accuracy, distinguish between different shades of organisational grey. Accordingly, it was the work of Greiner[32] which provided the necessary degree of analysis and gave rise to the questionnaire which we have subsequently called 'the organisational development diagnostic'.

With such an instrument available, it was then possible to proceed into the research, which comprised two phases:

1. application to the MBA case studies; and
2. wider application to companies to check the validity of the instrument to provide not only a diagnosis of the current situation, but also a prognosis about what issues needed to be addressed for future success.

Application to case studies

From an initial collection of some 50 case studies, which had been meticulously researched and written up for examination purposes by Cranfield MBA students, the researchers selected a sample of 34. These were chosen for further analysis because:

- they contained detailed information about the companies and the marketing planning procedures they used;
- they represented a broad cross-section of British industry in terms of the proportion of planners to non-planners; and
- they provided a wide spectrum in terms of company size, measured by the number of employees.

A breakdown of the research companies is provided in Table 4.2.

Assessing each company's stage of development against its approach to marketing planning provided the results shown in Table 4.3.

At a glance, it can be seen that planners are further along the biographical/maturity life line than semi-planners, who in turn lead non-planners. Equally, all planners appear to be experiencing a period of evolutionary growth.

Table 4.2 Research companies – an analysis

Description	No of companies	% of total
Non-planners: planning was non-existent or varied significantly from the process described in Figure 4.1	18	53.0%
Semi-planners: almost followed the planning process, but omitted one or two steps	9	26.5%
Planners: followed the complete planning process	7	20.5%

Table 4.3 Development phase versus marketing planning approach

	Type of planner		
Phase of development	*Non-planners*	*Semi-planners*	*Planners*
Creative evolution	XXXXXX		
Leadership crisis	XXXXX	X	
Directed evolution	XXX	XXXXX	XXX
Autonomy crisis		X	
Delegated evolution	XX	X	XX
Control crisis	X	X	
Coordinated evolution			XX
Red-tape crisis			
Collaborative evolution	X*		
Next crisis			
	18	9	7

Note: each company is represented by an X; * is a special case, a partnership

Interesting though these results were, it was felt that they might be inadvertently reflecting other factors which were not related to the 'phase of development' alone. Not least of these factors was company size. In other words, is the phase of development (and hence approach to marketing planning) really determined by size rather than a company's 'growth experience'? This objection could be easily tested, as Table 4.4 shows.

As can be seen, there is no neat correlation between phase of development and company size. Although in our sample a majority of non-planners were at the small end of the size spectrum, it was by no means conclusive. There were some non-planners at the 1000+ employee size. Therefore it would seem reasonable to conclude that phase of

Table 4.4 Phase of development versus company size

Phase of development	No of companies	Spread in size
Creative evolution	6	20–230 employees
Leadership crisis	6	70–3,000
Directed evolution	11	70–v. large
Autonomy crisis	1	800
Delegated evolution	5	50–v. large
Control crisis	2	350–v. large
Coordinated evolution	2	900–1000+
Red-tape crisis		
Collaborative evolution	1	50
Next crisis?		

development is not just a factor of size, but must also relate to other factors specific to each individual company.

In order to eliminate other possibilities, the case study companies' marketing planning procedures were considered against, (1) their rate of growth, and (2) the nature of their business. While the results of these comparisons were interesting, they did nothing to rock the initial findings, which showed a close correlation between a company's stage of development and its ability to adopt a comprehensive marketing planning process.

Sumary of case study analysis

The main findings from the analysis of the database companies were:

- planning companies were furthest down the track of organisational development, followed by semi-planners and finally the non-planners;
- the stage of a company's development did not necessarily equate to its size;
- a company's propensity to use marketing planning did not appear to be related to the growth of the business;
- the largest group in low growth businesses were non-planners;
- the nature of a company's business did not influence its likelihood of using a marketing planning process, but service companies seemed less likely to plan than manufacturing companies;
- there is a suggestion that manufacturing companies are more inclined to be in low growth businesses than service companies; and
- companies in fast moving goods or services are the most likely to use a complete marketing planning process.

Most importantly of all, this phase of the research had vindicated the organisational development diagnostic as a measuring instrument of some accuracy. It now remained to be seen if it would be equally proficient when tested out in 'live' companies.

Wider application to companies

Field research

Unlike its application to the case studies, where the researchers 'controlled' its completion, the organisational development diagnostic questionnaire was now completed by the top management team of the subject companies, or a cross-section of managers.

While one researcher examined the marketing planning processes of these companies, the other analysed the results from the questionnaires completely blind. That is to say, he had no knowledge of the company, its size, its business, location, or indeed who had completed the questionnaires, other than a brief indication about the person's function and level of management.

Analysis of the questionnaires

It was found to be essential that more than one person completed the questionnaire in any subject company, otherwise the results were highly skewed towards that person's perceptions of the organisation. Thus they painted a picture as much of the person as of the organisation.

Invariably, with several people completing the instrument, there were areas of consensus and also of disagreement. The researcher would base his diagnosis and prediction on those parts of the questionnaire where the company personnel had a high level of agreement. Indeed, having a number of responses from a single company provided a wealth of information offering a subtle undercurrent to the main findings, thus allowing for a richer and more accurate diagnosis.

The findings from the organisational development diagnostic were then written up in the form of a report to the company. Each report had two main sections:

1. A descriptive section which drew on the submissions from the company personnel and, from these, described the company's present stage of development.
2. An action-planning section which described whether or not it would be important for the company to take any immediate steps to recognise the onset of its next stage of development, and to adapt

accordingly. While there would be some generalisations about the organisation, the prediction tended to focus on what needed to be done in terms of improving marketing planning.

Reactions to the reports

Some 20 analyses have been completed and reports sent to the chief executives. Accompanying each report was a request for some feedback regarding the accuracy of the diagnosis, together with some comments about the usefulness of the proposed 'next steps'. In all of these reports, the diagnostic element has been judged as being reasonably accurate to highly perceptive.

However, reactions to the section about what to do next have been mixed. Most recipients tend to agree that the proposed steps are 'interesting' or 'sound useful', but there is little evidence that they are acted upon. Indeed one chief executive is known by the researchers to have valued the report, but to have kept it secret from his colleagues because of the 'political ramifications' of the proposed action steps.

Taken all round, it would seem that the organisational development diagnostic provides the information upon which an assessment can be made about an organisation's stage of development, and hence its marketing planning procedures. Moreover, based on our research the accuracy of such a diagnosis is quite high.

At an intellectual level, the accuracy of the prognosis might well rate similarly high. However, such a prognosis does not take into account whether or not there is the political will to take action on the recommendations. Without knowing more about the people involved and their preparedness to change, such a 'blind' analysis can do little more than flag the warning signals and point out what lies around the corner.

This work of assessing culture as a transitory step along a development continuum could be viewed as the macro perspective. However, the literature review also raised the issue about assessing culture by reference to the behaviour of the culture carriers, or what might, in comparison to the above, be termed the micro perspective. This was investigated in tandem with the research using the organisational development diagnostic.

The micro perspective

As an outsider, it was difficult to be sensitive to the culture signals sent out by the senior executive, to which the staff are so well attuned. Yet some mechanism was required to decode this information. The following line of reasoning led to a solution to this problem.

1. Culture carriers make clear their intent by the things they do and their general demeanour.
2. Subordinate managers will, on the whole, behave intelligently.
3. It is not intelligent to behave in ways which are contrary to the accepted culture.
4. Therefore managers behave in ways they believe they are expected to behave.
5. They are rewarded for exhibiting acceptable behaviour and so this becomes part of their repertoire.
6. Thus, an investigation into the ways that managers typically deal with day-to-day events should provide some insights into the prevailing company culture.

Experiments were made with several management style questionnaires and since their results correlated in a way hypothesised in the literature review, in reality any one of them would have been suitable. The decision was made to use a Blake-Mouton type of approach, and because this was most familiar to the researchers, an instrument was developed along these lines. It took the form of a questionnaire which could be interpreted against the typical grid structure shown in Figure 4.7. The scales on each axis were designated minimal (scoring 1) to high (scoring 9). The specially designed questionnaire enabled managers to identify their own positions on the grid. The position on the grid which predominated, when the results of a number of managers from the same company were taken together, was assumed to reflect something of the organisational culture.

With such scoring, grid positions are interpreted as follows:

- 1:1 style – low concern for both marketing planning and the contribution of managers;
- 1:9 style – low concern for planning coupled with a high concern for people;
- 9:1 style – high concern for planning, but low concern for people;
- 5:5 style – medium concern for both; and
- 9:9 style – high concern for both.

The results from the analysis of six companies using this questionnaire are shown in Table 4.5.

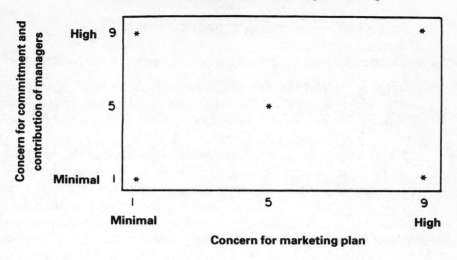

Figure 4.7 Management style grid

Table 4.5 Analysis of style scores

Company	Business	Style score	Planning category	Stage of development
1	Computers	9:1	Non-planner	Creative evolution
2	Training	1:9	Non-planner	Leadership crisis
3	Pens	9:1	Semi-planner	Directed evolution
4	Financial services	9:1	Semi-planner	Directed evolution/ autonomy crisis
5	Chemicals	9:9	Planner	Delegated evolution
6	Surveying	9:9	Planner	Collaborative evolution

It is difficult to draw firm conclusions from such a small sample of companies, except that the 'planners' exhibited 9:9 styles – ie a style which integrates the marketing planning process and the people involved.

Work is continuing using this instrument. There is a strong suspicion that it provides a guide to marketing planning as hypothesised in Figure 4.4, even though it does not as yet yield quite the same productive results as the organisational development diagnostic. None the less, this questionnaire is useful and is certainly capable of producing an interesting diagnosis of the company situation in a relatively quick and painless manner.

CONCLUSIONS

The thesis on which this chapter is based set out to test five hypotheses:

1. *A complete marketing planning process is not simply a series of action steps. It also embodies a set of values and assumptions which, while not being explicit, are nevertheless an integral part of the whole process.*

    This is certainly true. Furthermore there were strong clues from the analysis of the complete marketing planning process that companies best equipped to make the process work would be 'largely run on democratic principles, not be too hierarchical, be flexible rather than bureaucratic, use motivational mechanisms which promote openness and commitment to the organisation, have a collaborative climate which favours team-work, be interested in finding quality solutions when faced with problems, and have a genuine concern for providing customer satisfaction'.

    Clearly, such companies are relatively sophisticated and mature, when compared with a typical cross-section of their contemporaries. It also follows that by analysing the assumptions behind any company's marketing planning process, it ought to be possible to get closer to understanding its underlying beliefs and values.

2. *An organisation is not simply a conglomeration of people and resources. It embodies a set of values and assumptions which give rise to its distinctive corporate climate and culture. Moreover its culture would appear to be influenced to some degree by its level of learning or maturity.*

    Again, this hypothesis is true. Organisations, no matter how they are structured, never become inanimate machines. The people involved, their experience of the company's history, their own beliefs and values, all contribute to organisational life. This research has shown that as an organisation learns and moves along its biographical life line, different issues can exercise it at different life phases. In overcoming these issues, it in turn becomes more 'mature'. Equally, as we have seen, the culture carriers can be a power for change or stability, depending upon the values they make explicit by their behaviour (as opposed to those to which they publicly subscribe).

3. *If the underlying values of a complete marketing planning process are more or less consistent with those of the organisation, then there is a high probability that the planning process will be adopted.*

    It was found that the mature company, described under hypothesis 1 above, had an uncanny resemblance to the integrated organisation described by Lievegoed (1975)[33] and those at the more advanced stages of development put forward by Greiner (1972)[34] and many others.

The research conducted confirmed that planners were further along the development path than other companies. Other factors such as company size, nature of business, growth rate, and so on were checked in case they were hidden influences. However, within the bounds of this study, the original results held true. All this suggests that hypothesis 3 is correct.

4. *If there is a conflict of values between those underlying the complete marketing planning process and those of the organisation, then it could be expected that the planning process would be rejected*

From this research there were found to be a number of barriers to marketing planning, namely, cognitive, information, resource, behavioural and cultural. Therefore, a rejection of marketing planning could not be attributed to an organisation's cultural value system alone.

However, if an organisation made a genuine and determined attempt to introduce marketing planning, most of these barriers would not prove to be insurmountable. What the organisation would require, however, would be a level of maturity that doesn't come readily to all companies. For now, hypothesis 4 must remain unproven.

5. *An organisation will not change its values system or culture, unless something very significant takes place to make such a change seem worthwhile.*

All the works about change studied in the literature review confirmed this hypothesis. Schein (1985)[35] went as far as saying that corporate culture itself is the rock upon which change founders.

What might be termed significant will vary from organisation to organisation, but it will probably have to be something which is either unplanned or discontinuous, otherwise incrementalism will strive to neutralise its impact. Thus, intellectual curiosity on the part of the company would not appear to be a sufficient stimulus for introducing marketing planning, whereas falling sales or dwindling market share would be a different story. Equally, a new culture carrier championing marketing planning might prove to be the discontinuity to bring about change. However, as we have seen, the old culture would strive to maintain the status quo or to marginalise the change.

The question of change raises another interesting issue. Can the old culture carriers stay in command and introduce a new culture?

Evidence for this is very mixed. Perhaps a new organisational broom can sweep cleaner. The political nature of change ensures that there are no easy answers to the dilemma.

POSTSCRIPT

Throughout this research, a number of different 'flavours' of marketing planning were observed, all of which fell into the prescribed definition.

It is a tentative conclusion that a different style of marketing planning might be more appropriate according to where the company is on its development life line. In this sense, the planning approach can be modified to suit the corporate culture. Bearing in mind the relatively small sample of marketing planners, some speculative observations are presented in Table 4.6.

Table 4.6 Development phase and marketing planning

Phase of development	Type of planning process	Observations
Creative evolution	No planning found	Planning is counter-culture at this stage of development
Directed evolution	Centralised, tightly defined process, with a clear top-down direction	Works well if the system and instructions are clearly communicated and the business is not too volatile. The leader must demonstrate expertise.
Delegated evolution	Decentralised, less tightly defined process, relying on bottom-up contributions	High quality inputs, high staff morale and commitment, but the overall plan can lose focus
Coordinated evolution	Centralised planning, formal process, with clearly defined roles and responsibilities. Top-down and bottom-up direction	Makes good use of company specialists, but the plan can degenerate into a meaningless routine
Collaborative evolution	Reduction of bureaucratic processes. Creative solutions are found for resolving planning problems	Perhaps different planning processes for different product groups or markets. High concern for both people and the task of planning.

The thesis on which this chapter is based began by drawing attention to the low level of acceptance of marketing planning in British companies. This study now raises the following questions: (a) what sort of marketing planning are we talking about? and (b) what sort of company do we have in mind?

Marketing planning can range from the cosmetic to something of deep value to the company. Equally, companies range over a spectrum of different levels of development.

As we have seen, marketing planning is not a neatly packaged cognitive process. It is much more than this, and it brings the marketing adviser face-to-face with the political realities of corporate life. For his part, the chief executive will have to recognise that to introduce marketing planning successfully, many things will have to change within the organisation, not least, the way he behaves and the role model he sets for others.

REFERENCES

1. Thompson, S (1962) *How Companies Plan*, AMA Research Study, No 54, AMA.
2. Schoeffler, S, Buzzell, R and Heany, D (1974) 'Impact of strategic planning on profit performance', *Harvard Business Review*, March/April, pp 137–145.
3. McDonald, M H B (1984) *Theory and Practice of Marketing Planning for Industrial Goods in International Markets*, Cranfield Institute of Technology, PhD.
4. Greenley, G E (1985) 'Marketing plan utilisation', *Quarterly Review of Marketing*, 10(4), pp 12–19.
5. Leppard, J W (1987) *Marketing Planning and Corporate Culture*, Cranfield Institute of Technology, M. Phil.
6. Wills, G S (1976) *Business School Graffiti*, MCB Books, Bradford, Yorks.
7. Katz, R (1974) 'Skills of the effective administrator', *Harvard Business Review*, September/October, pp 90–102.
8. Boydell, T (1977) Paper presented at BACIE Conference, London.
9. Van Boeschoten, M (1975) Paper presented at 'Conference on Learning Situations', Hawkwood College, Stroud, Glos.
10. Glaser, B G and Strauss, A C (1967) *The Discovery of Grounded Theory – Strategies for Qualitative Research*, Aldine Publishing, New York.
11. McClintock, C C (1979) 'Applying the logic of sample surveys to qualitative case studies', *Administrative Science Quarterly*, December.
12. Camillus, J C (1975) 'Evaluating the benefits of long-range planning systems', *Long-range Planning*, June.
13. Ames, B C (1968) 'Marketing planning for industrial products', *Harvard Business Review*, September/October, pp 100–111.

14. Schein, E H (1983) 'The role of the founder in creating organisational climate', *Organizational Dynamics*, Summer.
15. Seymour, W D (1968) *Skills Analysis Training*, Pitman, London.
16. McDonald, M H B (1984) op cit.
17. Blake, R R and Mouton, J S (1964) *The Managerial Grid*, Gulf Publishing, Houston.
18. Lickert, R (1967) *The Human Organisation*, McGraw-Hill, New York.
19. Hersey, P and Blanchard, K H (1977) *Management of Organisational Behaviour*, Prentice-Hall, Englewood Cliffs NJ.
20. McClelland, D C (1970) 'The urge to achieve', in Kolb, D (ed) *Organisational Psychology*, Prentice-Hall, Englewood Cliffs NJ.
21. Lievegoed, B J C (1973) *The Developing Organisation*, Tavistock, London.
22. Greiner, L E (1972) 'Evolution and revolution as organisations grow', *Harvard Business Review*, July/August, pp 37–46.
23. Normann, R (1977) *Managing for Growth*, Wiley, Chichester.
24. Bhattachary, K (1981) *Financial Times* article, 27 November.
25. Burns, T and Stalker, G M (1961) *The Management of Innovation*, Social Science Paperbacks, Boulder CO.
26. Lawrence, P R and Lorsch, J W (1967) *Organisation and Environment*, Harvard School of Business Administration, Harvard.
27. Mangham, I (1979) *The Politics of Organisational Change*, Associated Business Press, London.
28. Marshall, J and McLean A (1985) *Current Research in Management*, Frances Pinter, London.
29. Johnson, G N (1984) *Managing Strategic Change – A Frames and Formulae Approach*, paper presented to the Strategic Management Society Conference, Philadelphia, October.
30. Williams, R C (1970) *An Exploration of the Change Agent and Client System Relationship in Planned Organisational Change*, Loughborough University Library, MSc.
31. Schein, E H (1985) *Organisation, Culture and Leadership*, Jossey-Bass, San Francisco.
32. Greiner, L E (1972) op cit.
33. Lievegoed, B J C (1973) op cit.
34. Greiner, L E (1972) op cit.
35. Schein, E H (1985) op cit.

5

The Role of Expert Computer Systems*

OVERVIEW

During the 1980s, Japanese activity in the field of expert systems and related technologies prompted the EC to give birth to the ESPRIT programme in an attempt to integrate European efforts. This in turn led to the DTI-sponsored ALVEY and IED programmes, and other initiatives. An outcrop of these is a DTI-sponsored club called EXMAR – comprising 10 major British companies. Formed in 1987, its objectives are to investigate the possibility of computerised assistance for strategic marketing planning by the development of a prototype, and to spread awareness of expert systems in club member organisations. It is funded by contributions from the member companies, and by the Department of Trade and Industry.

The purpose of this chapter is to examine the potential of expert systems, to outline the progress of the EXMAR project and to draw conclusions about appropriate computer support for marketing planning.

INTRODUCTION

A surprising fact about expert systems is that although they have inspired a number of new programming languages and powerful new computer

---

* Reproduced by permission of John Wiley & Sons, Ltd. This paper first appeared in the *British Journal of Management* volume 1, number 3, as 'State of the Art Developments in Expert Systems and Strategic Marketing Planning', copyright Professor David Otley.

architectures, they have made virtually no progress in the domain of marketing, and while most interested parties view them as a potentially powerful way of beating the competition, there are few products and no on-line systems available (Foster, 1985[1]; Moutinho and Paton, 1988[2]). Because artificial intelligence has become the latest buzzword, many software houses are hyping up their old software in advertisements, but most of these can be discounted as irrelevant in the real world of expert systems.

The principal reasons for this lack of progress revolve around the technical problems associated with getting computers to mimic experts and the costs involved. There are no shortcuts to building good expert systems. It takes a considerable amount of skill, patience and several years of effort to develop an expert system in a new area and get it into the field (Rangaswamy et al, 1988[3]).

WHAT ARE EXPERT SYSTEMS?

Expert systems are a branch of what is known as artificial intelligence, which is a loosely grouped activity in which a number of researchers of varying backgrounds have done some research since the mid-1950s. But artificial intelligence is still not tightly defined.

Conventional computing deals with simple and unambiguous facts with existing packages being little more than moronic number crunchers. Most software is written in the form of an algorithm, which is a list of commands for the computer to carry out in the order prescribed. It uses data held in a separate file, which is stored in a particular way. Thus, software is data plus algorithm and is useful for boring, repetitive, numerical tasks. The largest selling software has been spreadsheets and word processing packages. Database management was developed from this.

However, managers handle more than words and numbers. They are concerned about knowledge, which is information interpreted for a particular application. The British Computer Society definition of an expert system is:

> The embodiment within a computer of a knowledge-based component, from an expert skill, in such a form that the system can offer intelligent advice or take an intelligent decision about a processing function. A desirable additional characteristic, which many would consider fundamental, is the capability of the system, on demand, to justify its own line of reasoning in a manner directly attributable to the enquirer. The style adopted to attain these characteristics is rule-based programming.

Put more simply, expert systems capture not only the knowledge of a human expert, but also the rules he or she uses to reach conclusions. This knowledge is then made available to others by means of a computer program.

The two main components of an expert system are the knowledge base and the inference engine. The rules used by an expert and his knowledge and experience about a certain domain are interrogated and the captured knowledge becomes the knowledge base, which is the heart of the system.

The inference engine accesses the knowledge base, makes the necessary connections, draws conclusions, and generates the answers. The general reasoning strategies are separated from the knowledge base so as to allow the system to use knowledge in a variety of ways, requesting additional information if required to solve a particular problem and explaining the reasoning behind its questions and recommendations by reporting the rule and facts used. Since the knowledge base and inference engine are separate, an inference engine can be bought to be used in association with other databases. This is called a shell.

An expert system will usually have the following characteristics. It will:

- relate to one area of expertise or knowledge rather than to a set of data;
- be restricted to a particular topic;
- have collected the rules (heuristics) and knowledge of an expert;
- have an inference engine;
- be capable of extension;
- be able to cope with uncertainty;
- give advice; and
- explain its reasoning.

WHY HAS PROGRESS BEEN SO SLOW IN MARKETING?

During the 1960s, attention was focused on specific problem-solving applications in scientific fields. Many successful expert systems have been built, including MYCIN for diagnosing infectious diseases (Buchan and Shortcliffe, 1984[4]), and PROSPECTOR, a system for evaluating geographical locations for possible mineral deposits (Duda et al, 1979[5]).

Management problems, however, do not lend themselves to quite the same precise logic as scientific problems. People do not solve most of life's problems by mathematical means, but rather by experience, knowledge and intuition. Marketing problems are dealt with in the same way, as most of them are logical rather than mathematical, and problem-solving knowledge, while available, is incomplete.

Decision-support systems and the like use hard facts and static formulae which, given the correct data, provide correct answers. They belong more naturally to the logical, black-or-white, right-or-wrong world of computers. But managers in the world of marketing deal with uncertainties and often with vague concepts. Decisions invariably are built on a set of 'rules', or heuristics, that reflect the expert's own knowledge and experience about the problem in question. These rules are hard to specify and quantify, because the expert's experience enables him or her to think in terms of shades of grey, 'more or less', and 'approximately'. Such fuzzy reasoning is commonly used by human beings to find a path through situations that are too complex and amorphous for the human mind to handle in a totally conscious, rational, scientific way.

Most people would acknowledge that in virtually any walk of life, true experts have built their expertise largely from experience and an intuitive grasp of problem-solving in the real world, something which is often referred to as the 'University of Life'. Indeed, many of the world's leading business people acknowledge that they owe their success not to formal business education and text books, but to their own experience, flair and intuitive good judgment.

Schon (1984)[6] describes this phenomenon as follows: 'Competent practitioners usually know more than they can say. They exhibit a kind of knowing-in-practice, most of which is tacit'. He cites an investment banker, who makes his decisions based on 70 to 80 per cent instinct, and only 20 to 30 per cent calculable rules. This 'gut feel' was a major asset to the bank in question. His point is that artistry is not reducible to discernible routines.

He describes scientific rigour as 'describable, testable, replicable techniques derived from scientific research, based on knowledge that is testable, consensual, cumulative and convergent', but then goes on to argue that much of what passes for scientific management is irrelevant because business problems do not come well formed. Certainly, most marketing problems are messy and indeterminate and successful practitioners make judgements using criteria and rules which are difficult to define. Many academics would decry this as a lack of rigour, and in so doing exclude as non-rigorous much of what successful practitioners actually do.

Accounting for artistry

The problem to be addressed by expert systems in the marketing domain, then, revolves around how to take account of the intuitive artistry displayed by experts in situations of complexity and uncertainty in a way that is describable and susceptible to a kind of rigour that falls outside the boundaries of technical rationality. The question is, how an epistemology of practice can be captured and represented in an expert system.

For an expert system to mimic an expert, it needs to be able to deal with the uncertainties, complexities and vague concepts that human beings deal with routinely, even though such 'rules' are neither simple nor straightforward. For example, a simple rule for a marketing manager might be: 'If the market is growing, increase promotional expenditure'. This would appear to be easy for a human being to understand, but in reality words like 'market', 'growing', 'increase' and 'promotional expenditure' are open to many different interpretations, as indeed is the whole lexicon of marketing.

One way of dealing with this problem is the development of 'fuzzy sets'. A 'growing market', for example, is a fuzzy set in the sense that its meaning can vary from situation to situation. Fuzzy numbers approximate the response figures from marketing experts and these numbers are then loaded into, for example, sales projections and promotion analyses.

The foundation of any expert system is the knowledge base, which can be extracted from one or more experts in a particular field. The expertise is usually stored in the form of rules of thumb (heuristics), which are, typically 'If then' statements. For example, if A is true, then B is true; or if X is true, do Y. Given an initial set of circumstances, the system can map out a set of contingencies and further contingencies.

A heuristic differs from an algorithm in that it does not give a correct answer, nor does it guarantee results. It merely suggests a general direction that is more or less likely to prove more useful than another direction. An example of a heuristic in chess might be: 'If a player stays in control of the centre of the board, he or she is more likely to win'. In marketing, a heuristic might be: 'If the market is growing and if you have appropriate business strengths, then an appropriate marketing objective would be to grow market share'.

A system of interlinking heuristics in the form of a decision tree is one way of representing knowledge. These is sometimes 'backwards inferencing' and sometimes 'forward inferencing'. Backwards inferencing starts with an objective and tries different combinations of rules and/or actions until it is reached. Forward inferencing reasons from initial information until it reaches useful conclusions. This can give rise to what is termed 'combinatorial explosion', which can be avoided by pruning and the use of heuristics that are correct most of the time. This gives probable solutions to less rigorously defined problems that are too complex to be dealt with algorithmically.

To date, however, no one has seriously tackled the world of marketing with expert systems other than the MSI ADCAD (Rangaswamy *et al*, 1988[7]) system developed to advise on advertising design. After considering a variety of consumer and environmental factors, advertisers use a combination of empirical research, communication theory and rules of thumb to select communication objectives and select appropriate creative approaches.

The authors themselves list a number of weaknesses in ADCAD, but conclude: 'As one advertising executive put it: "it helps us to think a little deeper about the issues we have to consider in developing ads that are both strategically and executionally sound"'. Another interesting and relevant conclusion was that most managers, when asked, said they would like to make use of existing theoretical and empirical knowledge of marketing when making decisions. However, few actually did use such knowledge. Expert systems can bridge this gap by structuring, validating and disseminating marketing knowledge while, at a theoretical level, they challenge their creators to understand and critically evaluate the elements of marketing knowledge and their interrelationships.

In the next section, the approach taken to the analysis phase at the start of the EXMAR project is outlined, and the system objectives that were derived are described. The nature of the logical model that emerged is discussed, and the demonstrator system based on it is described, emphasising the nature and style of the support to the user provided by the system, how this reflects the logical model, and how this meets the system objectives.

EXMAR – PREVIOUS WORK AND EARLY OBSERVATIONS

The initial requirements analysis produced a number of interesting problems for the project, which were to sow the seeds of expensive and time-consuming delay. These problems can be summarized as follows:

- It became clear that not many of the member companies were particularly *au fait* with the methodology of marketing planning. This led to the problem of setting clear objectives for the project.
- The diversity of company industry types, ranging from capital goods to service industries, meant that no subsequent system could possibly be suitable for all circumstances.
- Problems and subsequent proposed objectives ranged from 'To support a formal planning framework to improve discipline during

the planning process' and 'To support further understanding of the effects of currency fluctuations' to 'To promote discipline in pricing control'.

For these reasons, it was decided to focus on the process of marketing planning itself rather than on any situation-specific system. A firm of software consultants was appointed project manager and a knowledge-based systems house was appointed principal contractor.

The systems house began a series of 12 half-day interviews with the author in order to develop a formal paper model as a basis for computerisation. Unfortunately, although taped and transcribed, they were largely unfocused due to the inexperience of the interviewers and little progress was made towards formal modelling of the marketing planning process. The problem centred around lack of proper project control by the project managers, confused expectations by members of the club based on marketing planning naivety, the inexperience of the knowledge engineers, and the passive role of the domain expert, which was necessary in view of the nature of the project.

The result was that the paper outlining the tasks to be performed by the computer system targeted the whole marketing planning process rather than any subset, and because of this breadth, the process to be computerised was not documented in any detail, nor backed up by any substantive models and interrelationships. Other specifications required by the development methodology in use, such as financial requirements, system structure and so on, were never produced.

New management

At this point, the project manager appointed new software consultants to take over the feasibility study and the delivery system. The new contractor set about finding some common requirements among end-users in order to outline the domain model, with a boundary definition showing which parts of the model would be tackled by the computer system. They set about establishing the following areas:

- scope;
- constraints;
- organisational impact;
- maintainability;
- extensibility;
- technology;
- time scales; and

- risk and cost versus quantifiable benefits.

Artificial Intelligence Ltd, the new software consultants, drew various conclusions about the appropriate technical approach.

The need for focus

The previous work had been on a broad front, involving analysis into all aspects of strategic marketing planning. This is a vast topic, tackling many of the most fundamental problems inherent in business activity, and progress was therefore slow. There was a need to focus on a subset of the overall problem.

Feasibility and utility to be established

The very title of the club, 'Expert Systems in Marketing', suggested that the use of expert systems techniques in this area was possible and appropriate. This assumption of feasibility was based on the observation that there existed demonstrable expertise, but why this might imply a classic rule-based expert system had not been addressed. This was a doubly large assumption as no previous systems (or work towards systems) were known in this application area. There was a need to address this early, as well as the related issue of how any system would be of use to the marketing planner.

Modelling and representation

It was decided that the appropriate first step was to carry out analysis in a closely scoped subset of the problem, with the emphasis on modelling the area using whatever formal techniques were appropriate. An example of the choices deliberately not made at the start was whether any modelling of expertise adopted the 'low road' of embedding the expertise in data structures and code, the 'high road' of an explicit, 'deep' representation, or the 'middle road' of an explicit but heuristic representation (Brown, 1984[8]). In this modelling work, the emphasis would be on representation rather than computation, as the essential first step towards any computer system.

The marketing swamp

Marketing will be referred to later in this chapter as a swamp of intuitive, experience-based practice with the occasional rocky peak of formal techniques. In the experience of Artificial Intelligence Ltd the best place to start when modelling such 'soft' domains was often on the boundary between the soft area and neighbouring more readily formalisable areas.

In this case, that meant starting with the established formal techniques and working out from there.

RESULTS OF ANALYSIS WORK – AND THE DEMONSTRATOR

Several analysis sessions were held with the author and with marketing practitioners in club member organisations. This resulted in an overall EXMAR system objective, an outline model that was used as the basis for a demonstrator system, and a list of areas where further work was required.

The overall EXMAR system objective was defined to be:

> To provide assistance for the marketing planning process in such a way as to spread knowledge and further understanding of how and why the various factors of the market interact and serve to define the parameters of the business activity.

The remainder of this section describes features of the model, and how these were exploited in the demonstrator. The structure is an interleaved description of the two. Each subsection describes a model feature and the relevant aspects of the demonstrator.

Assistance in interpretation and understanding

The model covers the data manipulated by a marketing planner when developing a strategic marketing plan, and structures the marketing planner's task. Many of the individual subtasks or processes of this task involve modelling by the user of the business context, or interpretation by the user of the information entered. There is much that a computer system based on the model cannot do for the user, and it became increasingly clear that its most appropriate aim is to assist.

The objective of the demonstrator was therefore to provide an interactive system that supports a marketing planner by providing tools that help the user to represent the state of the markets and products under consideration; to interpret this information so as to gain an understanding of the markets and one's place within them; and to determine a course of action based on this understanding.

Model of the process of generating a marketing plan

A hierarchical breakdown of the process the marketing planner should adopt to generate a marketing plan was defined. Encouraging the user to adopt this process is of value in itself, as the process incorporates much experience that helps avoid common pitfalls: for example, the need to arrive at an appropriate understanding of the current situation before setting objectives for the future.

The demonstrator uses this hierarchy as a basis for the user's navigation round the system. The initial screen display is shown to illustrate this (Figure 5.1). Also shown is a window for more detailed navigation round a particular stage.

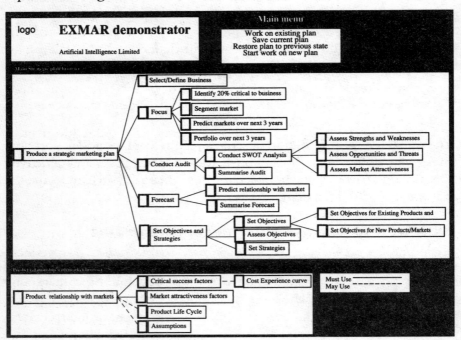

Figure 5.1 Initial screen display, with an example of a detailed browser

Each box in the graphical browser represents a stage of the process. The user carries out a stage by selecting a box with the mouse: the system then takes the appropriate action, which may, for example, be to present the user with a form to fill in, or to open a more detailed browser of the process for that stage.

To give an overview of the process, *Select/Define Business Unit* identifies which area of the business the marketing plan is for, and records the purpose of the business area. *Focus* identifies which of the unit's markets and products are of interest. *Conduct Audit* assesses the current position of the products and markets. *Forecast* predicts the future position of the products and markets, assuming we do not intervene, as a base-line for objective setting. Finally, *Set Objectives and Strategies* sets objectives for the business unit based on the information collected, analysed and summarised and defines strategies by which the objectives are to be met.

Detailed browsers contain icons showing the nature of the support offered for a particular stage: for example, there are icons for graphical displays of information, for tables of numbers, and for free text. The *Predict Relationship with Markets* browser is illustrated as an example, also in Figure 5.1.

Users will largely go through the process depth first and top-to-bottom; but they are free to do otherwise, as there are many cases where they may legitimately wish to do so.

A generally applicable, sound data model

A data model was developed that captured and related the information considered during production of a strategic marketing plan. It has proved essentially sound, and of general applicability to the wide range of marketing situations represented by the diverse club member companies. A simplified entity-relationship diagram of the model was included in Chapter 3 (see Figure 3.1).

The model has three cornerstone entities: *business unit*, the part of the organisation for which the plan is being developed; *product*, the products or services offered by the unit; *market*, the markets in which it operates.

Critical success factors model the workings of a market by document-ing the factors critical to the success of any product in the market, from the consumers' viewpoint. They are an objective assessment of how the market works, independently of the business unit's presence in it. The matching of products to markets is represented by the important 'product for market' entity: a product's score on the critical success factors relates to this entity.

Market attractiveness factors model the priorities of the business unit by documenting the factors determining how attractive a market is to the unit. Being a subjective assessment of the business unit's priorities, the criteria for their correctness must be the result of agreement between key executives. The matching of markets to business units is represented by the important 'involvement in market' entity: a market's score on the market attractiveness factors relates to this entity.

Time-dependent information is held in 'snapshot entities', which are 'forms' which must be completed by the user, whose role is to supply the relevant information such as product costs, prices, unit definitions, and so on. For each plan, the demonstrator system holds data structures closely based on the data model. The user's primary means of manipulating the data is by using these forms, one of which is illustrated in Figure 5.2.

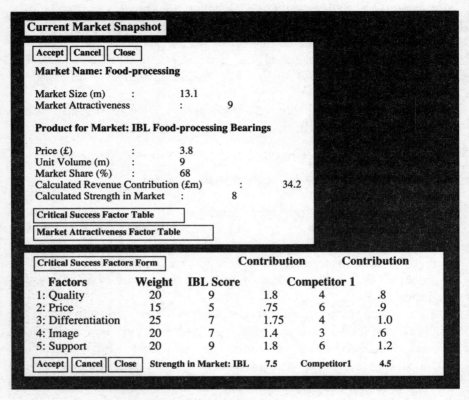

Figure 5.2 Typical forms for data notation

The top form shows current information about the food processing market for the fictional International Bearings Limited (IBL) company, which sells bearings into a variety of markets. The bottom form shows the critical success factors defined for this market, with weights to illustrate their relative importance. For example, while price is important in this market, it is less so than several other factors, such as product differentiation and quality, the product's image, and the engineering support provided. It also shows a score for IBL and its main competitor against these factors, and a weighted average computed by the system, to represent IBL's overall strength in the market. This is copied to the top form by the system. The market attractiveness score on the top form results from a similar weighted average form for the attractiveness of the market against such criteria as the market's size, growth and profitability.

The use of techniques in the data model

The 'rocky peaks' with which the analysis work started are 'textbook' techniques for analysing an organisation's markets and products, such as the directional policy matrix, which is illustrated in Figure 5.3, the Boston and Porter matrices, and so on. These view different aspects of the data model using differing graphical representations, to aid in interpretation of the data. To extend our analogy, the data model thus forms the bridges between the rocky peaks to enable us to navigate the intervening swamp.

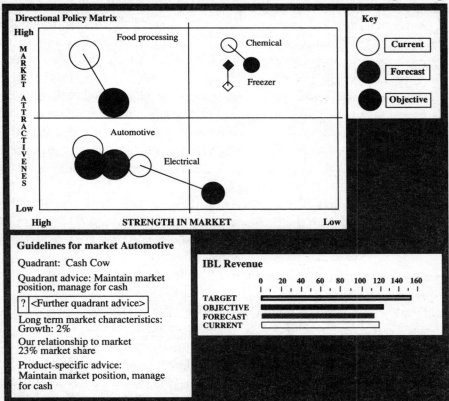

Figure 5.3 Data presentation to aid understanding

The screen snapshot in Figure 5.3 gives an example of how the demonstrator exploits these features by showing the underlying data presented in the standard formats. The directional policy matrix plots, for each of IBL's markets, the market attractiveness against IBL's strength in the market. The size of the circles is proportional to the market's contribution to IBL's revenue (though it could have been set to any useful metric). Different circle shadings illustrate the current, forecast and objective situations for the product/market. (In terms of the data model discussed earlier, each circle strictly represents a 'product-for-market'.)

The matrix aids in understanding both the situation of an individual product/market, and the balance of the portfolio of products. An example of the matrix's interpretation is that, in all its markets, IBL is moving downwards and rightwards from the current to the forecast situation. This indicates a general weakening of IBL's position: the matrix illustrates what IBL intends to do about this for the automotive market by maintaining its competitive position while cutting costs where possible.

On request, the demonstrator also provides standard, 'textbook' advice for a product-for-market in a given position on the matrix, as a guide to the planner in setting objectives. For example, for the automotive market, the system advises that the market position (strength in market and market share) be maintained, but that subject to this the market be managed for cash to fund development of more attractive markets. This is the only case in the demonstrator where it was felt appropriate that the system should take an active role of giving advice, rather than the passive role of presenting information in differing forms to aid the user in interpretation.

The diagram also shows a 'gap gauge' – a bar chart showing the financial gap between the business unit's target revenue and the sum of the individual objectives so far set for the various markets.

Less structured information: checklists and free text

Some parts of the marketing plan were best expressed in text: for example, the business unit's mission statement, and lists of opportunities and threats. Also, in several areas, marketing expertise was identified that was not formalised beyond free text in the model. Examples are checklists of common critical success factors; assistance with definition of a business unit's mission statement; and checklists of possible opportunities and threats to consider. This unstructured information was related, however, to specific points in the planning process, or to specific items in the data model. The demonstrator exploited this by making available text windows at appropriate points with icons on the browsers and elsewhere. This was implemented using the *NoteCards* hypertext system.

DEMONSTRATOR FEEDBACK AND THE DEVELOPMENT OF A PROTOTYPE

The demonstrator model was first seen by club members in December 1988 and was given unanimous acclaim by all. The following were the features which they especially recommended:

- The initiative is with the user – the demonstrator leaves the user to decide what to do next. This was liked by the club members, who felt it to be appropriate for this application.
- Evidence of utility – club members felt an operational system based on the demonstrator's ideas could be of significant use in the vital process of strategic marketing planning. This is an example of utility being addressed by the client rather than by the developers.
- Communication of the nature of the proposed prototype – the demonstrator served to communicate the nature of the support that would be offered to a marketing planner by a fuller computer system, to club members and to the author. With this innovative system, this was difficult to achieve on paper.
- Use in specification of prototype – the demonstrator was extremely effective in discussions with club members to aid with the specification of the prototype which was subsequently developed.

THE ROLE OF THE COMPUTER

The potential benefits shown by the EXMAR demonstrator are due mainly to its assistance with the understanding and interpretation of the information entered. The end results may include a marketing plan, but it also includes an enhanced and readily communicable understanding of the business gained by the marketing planner. These benefits are largely due to appropriate and varied display of the information.

Apart from data presentation, a computer system in this domain can perform the tasks for which computers have traditionally been used: managing data, maintaining constraints between data items like a spreadsheet, and performing routine calculations. These free up the user's thoughts for higher-level problems.

Finally, in some cases the computer can be more proactive, offering advice, pointing out decisions that go against conventional wisdom, and so on.

The most appropriate technology for this mix of roles will itself be a mix. In the case of EXMAR, the software techniques included object-oriented programming, hypertext and use of windows-based programming environments, to enable swift development and a carefully tailored user interface. We have not found rule-based representations so far to be relevant, though they may be in future developments.

To some expert systems workers this emphasis on data presentation and low-level data management, as opposed to sophisticated calculation or reasoning, would constitute some sort of failure. We consider, however, that the objective of computer systems is to make the combination of user and system more effective than the user alone, not to build 'clever' computer systems. Even in the classic scientific expert systems such as those quoted earlier, the user interface frequently constituted more of the work, and more importantly delivered more of the benefits, than emphasis in the literature would suggest. This may apply even more in such 'soft' and ill-understood areas as marketing planning. The rapid recent progress in the power, and price, of the underlying software tools that enable graphical user interfaces to be provided will ensure more such areas will be tackled effectively in the future.

Analysis approach

The analysis approach used for EXMAR was undogmatic and modest: to model the available expertise with whatever modelling techniques proved most appropriate, starting with the most well-established, documented and verified expertise. 'Don't run before you can walk' should not need emphasising, but the early experience of the club shows that perhaps it still does. The very term 'expert systems' has led some to unjustified assumptions not just about the feasibility of building computer systems based on expertise, but also of their utility and of the most appropriate modelling and system-building tools (Bobrow et al, 1986[9]). The alternative is classic software engineering, with an expanded tool kit of analysis and implementation techniques to draw upon as appropriate.

This may lead to the question about how and to what extent the model and demonstrator may be said to incorporate expertise. All aspects of the model and demonstrator can reasonably be said to be based on expertise: the process; the data model; the means of presentation of information; the checklists provided; and the one case where data-dependent advice is given. The system thus takes the 'low road' according to Brown's categorisation discussed earlier. There is certainly much available (but not necessarily formalisable) expertise that has not been captured. The critical design task has been the effective definition of the boundary between the system and the user such that the user is encouraged to think about the issues that the system cannot of itself address. This conforms to the stated EXMAR system objective quoted earlier, of providing assistance for the marketing planning process in such a way as to spread knowledge and further understanding of the business and its markets.

CONCLUSIONS

A number of conclusions can be drawn from the EXMAR experience:

1. The development of EXMAR shows that it is possible to use expert system methodologies to built support systems in complex areas of marketing management, especially if the domain is well defined, has a large number of factors to be considered and relevant expert knowledge is available.
2. The more complex and amorphous the expertise to be captured, the longer it takes both the expert and the knowledge engineer to reach an acceptable approximation. It is clear that to develop an expert system that is of some practical use requires both time and resources of massive proportions. This is supported by the MSI research paper[10] which concludes: 'There are no shortcuts to building a good expert system. It takes a considerable amount of skill, patience, and years of effort to develop an expert system in a new area and get it into the field'.
3. Expert systems provide a consistency to human decision-making which is valuable, since people tend to forget or ignore knowledge.
4. EXMAR has generated considerable interest and support among the major multinational companies that form the club, because it forces them to think deeply and in a structured way about the issues that need to be considered in developing a strategic marketing plan.
5. Expert systems are useful in helping both academics and practitioners to structure, validate and use marketing knowledge and to better understand the interrelationships between the elements of marketing.
6. Tight project control is vital. This view is supported by Mumford (1988).[11] Many issues need to be considered, such as clear definition of subject matter, availability of inputs, and clear agreement with users on objectives, timescales and resourcing. The close involvement of the EXMAR club members has been essential in this respect. It has been achieved through an active working party, through agreed quality assurance criteria for each stage of the work, and through the use of a demonstrator.
7. The potential advantages of expert systems in marketing are

consistent advice, secure knowledge bases, making better use of experts, enhanced decision making and improved analysis.

8. Since we live in an imperfect world, with imperfect problems and imperfect tools, it is unreasonable to expect a perfect expert system until there are perfect experts and perfect technology. On the other hand, if an expert system gives better advice than you would have had without it, it is probably worthwhile.

In conclusion, it is unlikely that expert systems will ever be able to give the same value as real human experts, although clearly they can offer reasonable advice. Nor will they guarantee that you make the right decisions. But they can help you gain a proper perspective of the alternatives.

In a sense, expert systems will always be a bit like distance learning programmes, which can replace a bad teacher, but never a good one.

REFERENCES

1. Foster, E (1985) 'Artificial intelligence', *Personal Computing*, April.
2. Moutinho, L and Paton, R (1988) 'Expert systems: a new tool in marketing', *Quarterly Review of Marketing*, Summer.
3. Rangaswamy, A, Burke, R A, Wind, J and Eliashberg, J (1988) *Expert Systems for Marketing*, Marketing Science Institution Working Paper Report Nos 87–107.
4. Buchan, B and Shortcliffe, E (1984) *Rule-based Expert Programs: The MYCIN Experiments of the Stanford Heuristic Programming Project*, Addison-Wesley, Reading MA.
5. Duda, R, Gaschning, J and Hart, P (1979) 'Model design in the PROSPECTOR consultant system for mineral exploration', in Michie, D (ed) *Expert Systems in the Microelectronic Age*, Edinburgh University Press, Edinburgh.
6. Schon, D (1984) *The Crisis of Professional Knowledge and the Pursuit of an Epistemology of Practice*, Paper for the Harvard Business School Colloquium on Teaching by the Case Method, April.
7. Rangaswamy, A, Burke, R A, Wind, J and Eliashberg, J (1988) op cit.
8. Brown, J S (1984) 'The low road, the middle road and the high road', in Winston, P H and Prendergast, K (eds) *The A1 Business*, MIT Press, Cambridge, Mass.
9. Bobrow, D G, Mittall, S and Stefik, M (1986) *Expert Systems: Perils and Promise*, Commun ACM, September, pp 880–894.
10. Rangaswamy, A, Burke, R A, Wind, J and Eliashberg, J (1988) op cit.
11. Mumford, E (1988) 'Designing computer-based systems', *University of Wales Business and Economics Review*, 3.

6

The Changing Face of Marketing in the 1990s

We have seen from earlier chapters that marketing planning is not fairyland textbook stuff, but a flesh-and-blood, real life struggle. Ego, greed, stupidity and other forms of human folly conspire to defeat the planner.

It is surprising, to say the least, when it is considered that research has shown a direct link between long-run profitability and an effective approach to marketing planning, that eight out of ten companies hardly bother with it at all, preferring to stick with forecasting, budgeting and financial husbandry.[1] Yet, the sheer speed of change, growing economic turbulence and intense global competition, make the task of forcing an organised approach to the identification of competitive advantage more pressing than it has ever been before. For, without competitive advantage, there will be no guaranteed growth in the 1990s and many more well-known names will disappear by the turn of the century.

This final chapter suggests some scenarios for the next few years on the way marketing is thought about and practised in companies.

MARKETING AND PROFIT

Although it has taken a very long time to begin to realise it, it is finally dawning on organisations that a tactical, short-term, purely financial approach, which seemed to work well in the past, no longer works. Of Tom Peters' 43 'excellent' companies, only 6 remain excellent at the time of writing (Pascale, 1990).[2] Of *Management Today's* top British companies over the past 11 years, only 5 are still profitable (Doyle, 1992).[3] Doyle's research in 1988 showed that almost 9 out of 10 British companies regarded short-term profits to be their main aim (compared with 80 per cent of US companies and only 27 per cent of Japanese companies).[4]

It will not have escaped the notice of the discerning observer of British industry, that exceptionally high profits today seem to be correlated with low or no profits tomorrow. Nor that the financial community has long recognised that short-run profits are a poor guide to shareholder value. Acounting practices are, of course, somewhat arbitrary, and short-run profits can be boosted, depending on how depreciation and stock valuation, acquisitions, foreign currency and research and development are handled. Financing growth through debt rather than through equity and boosting profits by trading off the future for the present (R&D, headcount, service and so on) always lead to growth in earnings per share, but a drop in the capital value of the shares due to the financial risks involved. The only conclusion that can be reached is that, contrary to popular belief, it is *managers*, not the financial institutions, that are short-term in their outlook.

All of this will have to change, however, otherwise the organisations that continue to espouse such outdated business management methods, will disappear in ever-increasing numbers. Companies will begin to measure *customer* profitability, as well as product profitability, as it is becoming increasingly obvious that it is the way we deal with customers that makes or loses us profit.

While this is not the place to raise the complex issue of how to treat intangible assets in the balance sheet, suffice it to say that with the compliance of the Accounting Standards Authority, more companies are beginning to place a value on their brand names. Some companies actually put this value in their balance sheets – a practice which the author believes is dangerous. A better practice by far, in the author's opinion, is to value intangible assets such as brands for the sole purpose of building them up and managing them appropriately. Marketing managers should be measured in terms of the return they get on these assets rather than on tangible assets.

Additionally, the overriding emphasis on return on sales as a measure of performance will be seen in a more well-balanced perspective. We all remember the basic accounting ratios set out in Figure 6.1.

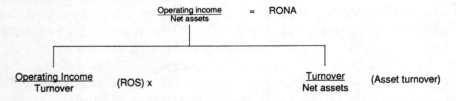

Figure 6.1 RONA, ROS and asset turnover

Quite simply, RONA measures how well an organisation is making use of the money invested in the business. It measures the annual trading profit (return), as a percentage of the investment in assets. Net assets are fixed assets (such as land, buildings, plant, machinery, furniture, cars, office equipment, etc) at their net book value, plus working capital employed (such as stocks, raw materials and work-in-progress plus debtors minus creditors). Understanding how working capital is used in the cash-to-cash cycle is key to improving RONA (see Figure 6.2).

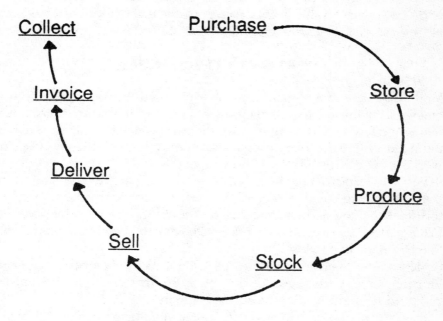

Figure 6.2 The cash-to-cash cycle

The distance round the circle, and the spaces between the steps, is the time it takes to achieve a return on the money invested in the business. So, the larger the circle, the longer it takes to complete the loop and the lower the RONA. By working to make the cash-to-cash cycle smaller, it is possible to move faster round the loop, making the money in the business work harder and harder and more efficiently to generate a better RONA.

While all of this may seem obvious, it is none the less surprising that so many organisations still place too much emphasis on the first part of the equation – ie return on sales (margin) – and not enough on asset turnover, for, clearly, a better result may be obtained by accepting a lower ROS and gaining a higher asset turnover. The truth, of course, is that organisations need to concentrate on both sides of the equation. For example, working capital can be tightened by reducing surplus raw material stocks, manufacturing on a just-in-time basis, and only stocking what is essential to deliver on time and in full. Margin can be improved by cutting out waste, by reducing non-essential costs and by selling higher value goods and services to meet customer needs.

The main point is that looking at the absolute profitability of individual products and services and making management decisions about important issues such as product launches, product deletions, promotional effort and so on is unlikely to be as acceptable in the future as it has been in the past. This raises the important issue of portfolio approaches.

PORTFOLIO APPROACHES

More than any other management tool, portfolio management will emerge as being key to an organisation's success. It is clear, for instance, that while few would disagree with the fundamental common sense of the need to balance margin and asset turnover, the difficulty arises in working out exactly when and how to do this.

For a full and detailed methodological approach to the subject of portfolio management, readers should refer to a paper by the author.[5] In this final chapter, all that is necessary is to review briefly why portfolio management is so important in relation to what has been said thus far and in relation to what follows.

Most readers will recognise the box in Figure 6.3, developed by General Electric some years ago. It can be seen that they used *industry attractiveness* and *business strengths* as the main axes.

It is not necessary, however, to use a nine-box matrix, and many managers prefer to use a four-box matrix similar to the Boston box. Indeed this is the author's preferred methodology as it seems to be more easily understood by, and useful to, practising managers. The four-box directional policy matrix is shown in Figure 6.4. Here, the circles represent sales into an industry, market or segment and, in the same way as in the Boston matrix, each is proportional to that segment's contribution to turnover.

The difference in this case is that rather than using only two variables, the criteria which are used for each axis are totally relevant and specific to each company using the matrix. It shows:

- markets categorised on a scale of attractiveness to the firm;
- the firm's relative strengths in each of these markets; and
- the relative importance of each market.

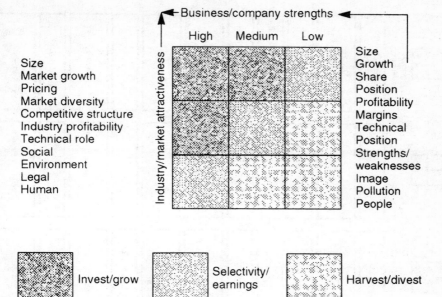

Size
Market growth
Pricing
Market diversity
Competitive structure
Industry profitability
Technical role
Social
Environment
Legal
Human

Size
Growth
Share
Position
Profitability
Margins
Technical
Position
Strengths/
weaknesses
Image
Pollution
People

Invest/grow

Selectivity/
earnings

Harvest/divest

Figure 6.3 General Electric's matrix

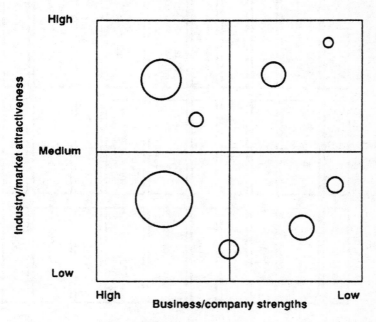

Figure 6.4 A four-box matrix

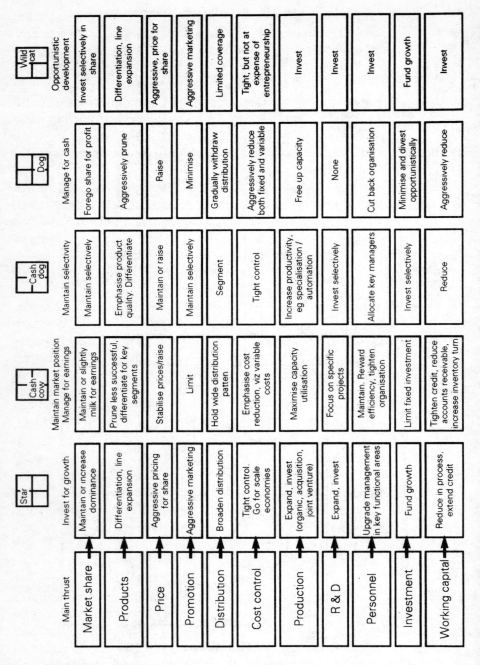

Main thrust	Star — Invest for growth	Cash cow — Maintain market position / Manage for earnings	Cash dog — Maintain selectivity	Dog — Manage for cash	Wild cat — Opportunistic development
Market share	Maintain or increase dominance	Maintain or slightly milk for earnings	Maintain selectively	Forego share for profit	Invest selectively in share
Products	Differentiation, line expansion	Prune less successful, differentiate for key segments	Emphasise product quality. Differentiate	Aggressively prune	Differentiation, line expansion
Price	Aggressive pricing for share	Stabilise prices/raise	Maintain or raise	Raise	Aggressive, price for share
Promotion	Aggressive marketing	Limit	Maintain selectively	Minimise	Aggressive marketing
Distribution	Broaden distribution	Hold wide distribution patten	Segment	Gradually withdraw distribution	Limited coverage
Cost control	Tight control. Go for scale economies	Emphasise cost reduction, viz variable costs	Tight control	Aggressively reduce both fixed and variable	Tight, but not at expense of entrepreneurship
Production	Expand, invest (organic, acquisition, joint venture)	Maximise capacity utilisation	Increase productivity, eg specialisation / automation	Free up capacity	Invest
R & D	Expand, invest	Focus on specific projects	Invest selectively	None	Invest
Personnel	Upgrade management in key functional areas	Maintain. Reward efficiency, tighten organisation	Allocate key managers	Cut back organisation	Invest
Investment	Fund growth	Limit fixed investment	Invest selectively	Minimise and divest opportunistically	Fund growth
Working capital	Reduce in process, extend credit	Tighten credit, reduce accounts receivable, increase inventory turn	Reduce	Aggressively reduce	Invest

Figure 6.5 Guidlines for setting objectives and strategies

When executives begin to think clearly about the criteria for judging the relative potential of each of their markets, products, regions, countries, distributors (or whatever) in achieving their growth and profit objectives, it becomes clear that there is a logical pecking order. It also becomes clear that the ones with less potential for growth are often the ones that provide much of the profit today, while the ones with more potential for the future still require some considerable effort and investment to build up or to keep good positions in these attractive, growing 'markets.' Equally, it becomes clear that in some of these 'markets', organisations have greater strengths than in others.

This categorisation into four boxes has wide-ranging implications for any organisation, in terms of its personnel, production, R&D, distribution, finance and, most of all, marketing. The 'guidelines' in Figure 6.5 indicate some of the more obvious considerations that should be taken account of in setting objectives and strategies for each of the organisation's 'markets', depending on where they are positioned in their four-box directional policy matrix.

When categorised thus, there is no problem in deciding, for example, when the focus should be on ROS as opposed to asset turnover, where problems should be treated as marketing problems, what kind of people to put into different roles, when to be tough or flexible on credit control, where to direct the advertising and selling effort and so on.

Alas, too many organisations preface their actions with the phrase 'Our policy is . . .' which really means that they treat all 'markets' in more or less the same way and use the same financial measures of efficacy for all, 'shooting themselves in the foot' in the process.

The author's prediction, then, is that there will, of necessity, be a much greater sense of portfolio and that appropriate policies will be developed that reflect the market position and the organisation's strengths. Only in this way will the crude, short-term financial husbandry that has decimated British industry be replaced.

MARKETING AND INFORMATION TECHNOLOGY

Billions of pounds have been spent on information technology (IT) during the past two decades, most of it with little effect. Departmental, or functional, problems have attracted swarms of IT providers, all keen to solve the problem with yet more 'tin'. Each project has been justified in ROI terms, usually in the form of number of bodies saved, with little or no post-investment check on the actual ROI. Another feature of this contagious IT disease has been the fragmentation of information systems

(IS), with little interconnection between one departmental IT solution and another.

All this has succeeded in doing is to focus the hearts and minds of managers more on their narrow departmental interests and away from the correct organisational focus – customers. The author predicts that customer market focus will surface in a way never experienced before, with real bonding between supplier and customer. For this to happen, companies are already beginning to realise that they need a complete overhaul of their IS and IT strategies, which will have to be based on the key issues that emerge from a genuine desire to be customer responsive.

This will inevitably mean breaking down the functional barriers and building IS and IT systems that are much more future orientated than financially driven.

MARKETING QUALITY

Marketing will no longer be only a function within the organisation. There will be an attitude of mind which uses all the appropriate marketing artefacts to build relationships, not only with customers, but with suppliers, shareholders, financial institutions, employees and, above all, internal customers.

Already, leading companies like Rank Xerox, Procter and Gamble, 3M and General Electric are using competitive benchmarking to monitor the best operators in any function, in any industry, anywhere in the world, in order to transfer best practice into their own internal operations. They are doing this as part of a relentless drive to give customers a better deal.

It is unfortunate that much of what passes for total quality is internally orientated, with little reference to the customer. Up to now, quality in the main has referred to operations, and in particular to manufacturing. Such laudable initiatives, driven by BS 5750, ISO 9000 and ES 29000 have had a beneficial effect on product quality, but have achieved little for the customer. Customers demand and should, by rights, receive, flawless products. All of this is to little avail, however, if such quality initiatives are internally driven. Product quality in its broader sense involves much more than the tangible product, as can be seen from Figure 6.6.

Unfortunately, real customer need has been excluded from much of the extant legislation. As can be seen from Figure 6.7, none of the existing standards tackle the real issues surrounding customer need. It is only the shaded area that is covered by existing legislation.

The author predicts that the tentative start made by Marketing Quality Assurance (MQA) in defining international standards for marketing

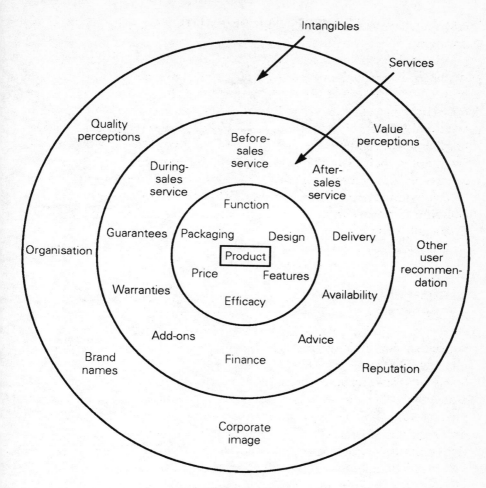

Figure 6.6 Product quality

quality, will drive a whole new code of behaviour in relation to the way companies treat customers. This organisation, with an independent governing board, has defined 35 standards for marketing quality, under the three key headings shown in Table 6.1.

It is clear to the author that, before long, companies that cannot demonstrate that they have achieved an independent international standard in relation to marketing, will not be able to deal with the world's leading companies.

THE PURSUIT OF QUALITY

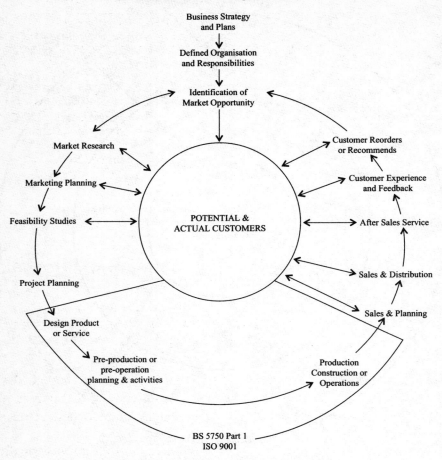

Figure 6.7 The pursuit of quality

Table 6.1 MQA specification – The three key areas

Customer focus	Business, marketing and sales plans	Management responsibility
• Continually identifying and reassessing customer needs, preferences and competition	• Business plans – strategy – customer input • Marketing and sales plans	• Quality policy • Organisation • Management review • Quality systems
• New products, meeting customer requirements, market readiness	– marketing audits – objectives/strategies – role of contributing departments	• Resources, personnel, training • Controls and procedures
• Customer communications, care information, monitoring and feedback	• Marketing and sales operations • Performance measurement	
• Customer support programmes	• Purchasing • Administration	
– after-sales service	• Contributing depts.	
• Code of conduct		

PROFESSIONAL MARKETING

Throughout this book, frequent reference has been made to the fact that few organisations use any of the well-known tools and techniques of marketing. This is largely because so few marketing managers actually understand how to use them in a technical sense.

It is a pity that few practising marketing managers are professionally qualified, a situation which, until it is rectified, will lead to the supremacy of finance and accounting and the subservience of marketing as a discipline. The Diploma of the Chartered Institute of Marketing will become an essential starting point in a marketing career, with BA, BSc and MBA degrees with a marketing specialisation becoming the norm. Only when most people holding a marketing job hold a professional qualification will marketing as a function be truly elevated to its rightful position alongside finance, personnel and production. Such people will need to be excellent communicators, politicians, and general managers, as well as excellent marketing practitioners, as marketing will occupy a much more central role than hitherto, with marketing as a concept and a code of behaviour driving the organisation.

As already stated in Chapter 5, computers will become a more accepted part of marketing. In particular, expert systems and knowledge-based systems will bring marketing techniques within the marketing office, so that they become a part of everyday life rather than being confined to textbooks and courses.

ORGANISATION

The author was recently asked to run a series of in-house marketing programmes for a major global company that had narrowly avoided a hostile takeover. Its shares had consistently underperformed the FTSE average. The chairman decided that his company should be more market-orientated, and marketing programmes were to be a significant part of the change process.

One such event revolved around the important subject of marketing creativity. Yet, the expressions of fathomless vacuity on the faces of participants revealed a massive disjuncture between the aims and content of the course and the deeply hierarchical structure within the organisation that penalised initiative, rewarded compliance and subservience, and discouraged anyone but the most senior managers from using their initiative.

Facing this situation, managers on such a course would clearly be stupid to change their behaviour, as to do so would lead to punishment. The result, of course, was that they paid lipservice to the course, and no tutor, no matter how skilled, could possibly succeed.

Likewise, as organisations are essentially political structures, in which groups of people acquire, wield and defend power aggressively in highly specialised groups, or departments, it is unlikely that another, probably newer, marketing department, would have much influence or sway over the company's strategy. Accountants are unlikely to publicise the irrelevancy of much of the information produced by their systems. IT departments are unlikely to admit that they have contributed absolutely nothing to the customer's or to the company's prosperity. Personnel are hardly likely to admit to failing to respond effectively to the company's changed environment. Nor are production people likely to admit that their preoccupation with MRP 2, Right-first-Time, Just-in-Time programmes, and the like, often have little to do with anything that is of relevance to the customer.

The result of all this is that organisations build up a resistance to the marketing concept by dint of their sectionalisation. 'Marketing' becomes a political process, which is rejected by sectional interests striving to retain their power bases. Hence, new procedures, structures and frameworks introduced by marketers designed to deliver greater customer satisfaction, are viewed as political processes which are likely to weaken sectional interests and power bases and are, therefore, rejected. An example of this is the introduction of marketing planning procedures involving the formalisation of data and information initiated by managers in a central marketing department. Resistance has got very little to do with rationality. Resistance is based on the subsidiary's conviction that such procedures hand power and control to the marketing department. The marketing department is perceived as having their own agenda, their own powerseeking goals, and their own values, all of which is to do with spreading marketing influence and power and reducing their own priorities and values. The result is that such procedures are rejected as being irrelevant, and a 'battle' starts, in which sectional interests are preserved, priorities protected, departmental culture defended, goals justified and budgets and priorities fought for, all of this being related much more closely to departmental objectives than to the interests of the customer. All new initiatives, therefore, and especially marketing initiatives, are viewed as a weakening of the traditional power base.

It is hardly surprising, then, that the pristine concepts, tools and techniques of marketing taught on marketing courses and written about so profusely in books, take a back seat in such an organisational milieu and are rarely used.

Finally, then, organisational structures will change from their narrow, functional focus, to being orientated towards customers. Teams consisting of managers from several disciplines will focus on customers and markets, so that accountants, for example, will be fighting on behalf of customers rather than on behalf of their functional discipline.

CONCLUSION – THE FUTURE OF MARKETING

This chapter has attempted to explain why there is such a huge gap between the theory of marketing as taught in universities and what actually happens in the real world. In doing so, many criticisms were levelled at the current state of affairs, and some suggestions were put forward about how some of these barriers can be overcome.

The author has little doubt that attitudes in industry are slowly but surely changing towards marketing, largely as a result of the traumatic market conditions of the past two years, which have forced many well-known companies out of business. Those remaining are beginning to take a cautious look at marketing once again. In future, however, the new breed of marketing director will play a central role in steering the organisation towards the most promising fields. The role of the marketing director has gradually changed from being a dispenser of largesse to grateful consumers to that of a fighter for the consumer's attention. Somewhere along the line, however, the battles for the hearts and minds of his own financial, technical and production people in the difficult process of gaining a sustainable competitive advantage have been lost, and he has often ended up on his own – misunderstood, pilloried and eventually dismissed.

The 1990s, however, will see the emergence of the marketing director to the central, starring role. But he will need to change his ways. Gone are the days when senior company personnel could afford to confuse marketing with sales, product management, advertising, and market research. There are still a lot of these characters around, of course, but they will not get very far during the 1990s. The danger of confusing marketing with the American 'Have a nice day' syndrome will soon pass as companies come to realise that they have to get *all* the elements of the offer right to succeed.

People still look incredulously towards the Japanese, even though it is obvious that all they have ever done is to provide value for money by getting all the elements of the offer right, and that everyone in the organisation understands that their success depends on customer satisfaction.

The marketing director of the 1990s, therefore, will have to be a person of both stature and intellect, with appropriate professional marketing training, not a reject from other functions. Marketing is increasingly about focus and concentration. This means an on-going dialogue with specific groups of customers, whose needs we must understand in depth, and for whom better offers are developed than those of competitors. A marketing man or woman should only shout when there is something to shout about.

The marketing director will play a central role in directing the organisation's strengths towards the most promising opportunities. He will also have to understand the real meaning of profit, rather than the very narrow financial definition imposed on organisations by accountants. Return on sales, cash flow, net present values, return on investment, asset turnover, and the like, can be disastrous if applied equally to everything that moves in an organisation. So the marketing director will have to have a deep understanding of the significance of portfolios of products and markets and the different policies that emanate from them.

The marketing director will also have to understand the real meaning of intangible assets. Companies are only beginning to realise that much of what appears on their balance sheets is rubbish and that it is brand names and relationships with customers that make profits, not factories and tangible assets.

In addition, the marketing director will have to learn to think strategically rather than being a tactical marketing technician – the preferred mode to date. He will have to learn how to use the principal marketing planning tools to help create a sustainable competitive advantage and to develop 'global fortresses' for his main products. The entrenched tribal mentality endemic in organisation charts, most of which is alien to the notion of satisfying customer need, must be overcome. In doing so, the marketer will have to redefine his strategic business units around customers rather than around products, functions, or geography.

The marketing director will also need to get a much better handle on marketing information about the principal determinants of commercial success (ie the business environment, the market, competitors, and himself). In doing so, he will need to understand better what information technology can do for him. For example, the leaders will surely be developing expert marketing systems (EMS) so that the best marketing expertise in the company can be applied by all executives anywhere in the world, rather than being hoarded inside the heads of a few gifted individuals.

He will need to think globally. This will entail developing the right skills in all executives involved in marketing, developing the systems to focus on the right issues, and being able to aggregate and synthesise what is fed into global strategies. He will then need to ensure correct priority of objectives and resource allocation. He will also need to recruit properly qualified chartered markerters (the Institute of Marketing is now Chartered).

Last, he will have to improve dramatically his communication and political skills. General management skills will also be important, and it is unlikely that anyone not educated to at least MBA standard will succeed.

If all of this is to come to pass, it can be seen that there will be an increasingly major role to be played by marketing teachers. In the UK, we have more than our fair share of world-class educators, as well as a solid base of rising stars. The author's advice to those who will continue to take the brunt of the marketing education workload in the future is:

- acquire a totally sound theoretical knowledge base in marketing;
- try to have an even greater in-depth knowledge of certain aspects of marketing;
- acquire a thorough understanding of other disciplines and where marketing 'fits in';

- use and develop innovative teaching/learning methods;
- get the teaching balance right between knowledge, skills, and attitudes;
- don't believe the saying, 'Those who can, do. Those who can't, teach'. Teaching is a wholly professional job requiring finely honed skills. You don't need to be a millionaire to be a successful marketing teacher; and
- above all, persevere in what will increasingly be a challenging and rewarding profession.

Table 6.2 summarises marketing trends during the past 30 years and summarises the author's prognosis for the remainder of the 1990s.

Table 6.2   Marketing evolution

	1960s	*1970s*	*1980s*	*1990s*
Economy	Growth	Crisis	Flat	Instability • Rapid change • Increased competitiveness (1992)
Product marketing	Brand proliferation	Brand rationalisation	Polarisation	Globalisation • Major brands • Major segments • Major customers • New product development
Consumer requirement	Choice	Price/value	Identity	Service • Quality • Impact of technology
Profit source	Market expansion	Margin improvement	Share shift	Added values • Productivity
Strategy	Diversification	Resource allocation	Competitive strategy	Marketing management • Global integration • Intrapreneurship • Customer/ market force

What to do to succeed

In conclusion, the author offers his views on the key change areas in the 1990s, especially those relating to the new Europe, as well as the implications for corporate responses.

Key change areas – the new Europe

End-users
Will our current customer base increase or decrease in numbers, change its purchasing policies, demand different levels of customer service? For example, a movement towards pan-European buying and a change of public procurement practices.

Pricing
How will the likely movement towards pan-European price harmonisation affect us and what will be the effects of trying to maintain price differentiation? For example, growth of international purchasing, stimulation of transnational distribution and expansion of parallel trade.

Distribution
How will the structure and nature of our distribution networks be affected by changing patterns of end-user purchasing, price harmonisation and product availability? For example, fewer, larger distributors, pan-European distribution and increasing demand for distributor own-branding.

Products
How far will our product portfolio be affected by EC legislation and the changing needs of end-users and distributors? For example, EC legislation on specifications, certification, patents and trademarks and demands for common product and service standards.

Competition
What are the likely scenarios post-1992 for current competitors, potential EC competitors and competitors from other parts of the world, notably USA and the Far East? For example, will the future market environment play to the strengths and weaknesses of these different competitive forces and what will their strategies be?

Corporate response – the new Europe

Strategic implications
Will the key service factors for competitive advantage be changed for or against us as a result of 1992? Should we modify our corporate goals and

strategies to take advantage or better defend ourselves in the light of our analysis of the key change areas?

Marketing activities

Are our current databases on end-users, distributors and competitors adequate to enable accurate planning and decision-making? What do we need to do to improve existing products and develop new ones to satisfy a coalescing European market? How can we construct a coherent European pricing strategy recognising the pressure towards harmonisation yet the differences in national customer service costs? How should our marketing communications policy be developed to balance pan-European and local positioning needs through the use of PR, advertising and sales promotion?

Sales activities

How should our key account sales effort be changed to handle larger, pan-European purchasers and the changing requirements of public procurement? What sort of sales-forces will be needed to market through the changing distribution networks? What are the implications of these changes for the numbers, knowledge, skills and attitudes of salespeople and what new policies do we need for their recruitment, training and motivation? Will the nature and scale of sales support need to be changed in terms of the sales office, after-sales service and technical advice?

Organisation

What new tasks need to be performed and thus what human resources will be required to handle pan-European end-users and distributors and to develop consistent product portfolios, pricing and communication programmes? How should these activities be best managed in the future? Do 'home and export' or 'multinational' structures have any relevance in a unifying European market?

Ten factors for success in the 1990s

1. **Environmental sensitivity**
   The 1990s are different from any other decade. Continuously monitor and understand the changes that are taking place in your own *external environment* (opportunities and threats).

2. **Competitive analysis**
   Continuously monitor competitors' strengths and weaknesses in each segment in which you compete.

3. **Internal sensitivity**

   Carry out a formal *position audit* of your own strengths and weaknesses, particularly your own *product/market* position in each segment in which you compete (strengths and weaknesses).

4. **Understand the sources of competitive advantage in total and by segment**

   Overall competitive advantage is gained by a deep understanding of the needs of specific customer groups, for whom you develop specific offers that have a differential advantage over the offers of competitors.

5. **Understand your portfolio** (of products and markets)

   You cannot be 'all things to all men'. A deep understanding of portfolio analysis will enable you to allocate your resources appropriately and to set appropriate marketing objectives.

6. **Develop clear strategic priorities**

   Focus your very best resources on the best opportunities for achieving long-term growth in revenue and profits.

7. **Be disciplined**

   Manage the economics of your business with an unrelenting discipline that focuses on the key performance indicators in relation to your strategic priorities.

8. **Customer orientation in all functions**

   Ensure that every function in the organisation understands and believes that they are there to serve the customer, not their own narrow, functional interests.

9. **Commitment to innovation**

   Continuously strive to serve customer needs better. This means being innovative.

10. **Leadership**

    Do not let doom and gloom pervade your thinking. The hostile environment offers many opportunities for companies with toughness and insight. Above all, lead the management team *strongly*. Don't accept poor performance in the most critical positions.

REFERENCES

1. Greenley, G (1989) 'An exposition into empirical research into marketing planning', *Journal of Marketing Management*, July.
2. Pascale, RT (1990) *Managing on the Edge: How Successful Companies Use Conflict to Stay Ahead*, Viking, London.
3. Doyle, P (1992) 'What makes an excellent company?', *Journal of Marketing Management*, Spring.
4. Wong, V, Saunders, J and Doyle, P (1988) 'The quality of British marketing: a comparative investigation of international competition in the UK market', *Proceedings of the 21st Annual Conference of Marketing Education Group*, Huddersfield Polytechnic, July, Butterworth-Heinemann, Oxford.
5. McDonald, M H B (1990) 'Some methodological problems associated with the directional policy matrix', *MBA Review*, Spring.

INDEX